Power'n 24/7 Praise

Janice Revels

Published by Purpose Publishing
1503 Main Street #168 • Grandview, Missouri
www.purposepublishing.com

ISBN: 978-09858266-6-6

Copyright © 2013, Janice Revels

Cover design by: Sharon Dailey
Editing by: Frank Kresen

Printed in the United States of America

This book, or parts thereof, may not be reproduced, stored in a retrieval system, or transmitted in any form or by means – electronic, mechanical, photocopy, recording, or any other without the prior permission of the publisher.

This book is available at quantity discounts for bulk purchases. Inquiries may be addressed to:
www.JANICEREVELS.com

Scripture used in this book are noted from the KJV of the Bible

Preface

Why would I
someone who is in no way noteworthy
think anyone would be remotely interested in reading a book
about my life?
I don't have a bachelor's degree and I am only now
at the age of 58
pursuing a two-year certificate as an
Administrative Support Assistant.
I ponder this question with intense, analytic consideration.
My answer:
The blessing of God compels me.
I am compelled to share
how and why my seemly uneventful, average life
has been and is so incredibly meaningful!
What's for you to gain by reading this book?
The understanding of how
God can be a very prominent presence in your life,
no matter what your circumstances are.

Dedicated to

My beloved children, for their eternal, loving encouragement and support, Charlotte, Carla, Caira, Russell, and Ricky, and my loving parents, Clifford and Angie Lee,
and Karen Johnson, my beloved sister, for spiritual encouragement and support.

Acknowledgements

My Heavenly Father, whose Spirit of love covers me as a blanket of warmth on a cold night.

Russell Revels for being a tenacious marketing manager.

My friends, who dare to take the first look
into the very rough draft and whose
continual enthusiasm and
encouragement took me a little further.

Rona Morrow and Shanae Alston

To my publisher and all comprising
Purpose Publishing who were patient and kind
in keeping me on target as I
muddled through my first book.

Table of Contents

Introduction..13

Part I:
Will I Praise You, Lord, for All of Days? 17
Back to the Black..19

The Silent Destroyer/The Great Restorer..........................27

How Bright, the Dark, Cloudy Days* 28

Youthful Encounter...29

Abuse — from the Outside Looking In*.............................35

Part II:
Will I Praise You, Lord, for Keeping Me in Your Way?..37
Not Always Pure and Righteous....................................39

Reaping*...46

Old Days, New Ways...47

New Life In Christ*..52

Busy Loving You, Lord*...53

Uh-uh! No Way!*..54

Part III:
Will I Praise You, Lord, for Blessings From Above? 55

Crazy Chimes..57

Searched and Found...59

Life*...65

A Unique Privilege..81

Old Soldiers*...86

Death...87

Reality*..93

Ricky*..94

Part IV:
Will I Thank You for Your Mercies and Thank You for Your Love? 95

Solace of an Old Friend......................................97

Sweet Hour of Prayer Poem* 100

Thank God, Not Like Job......................................101

I Am Healed, Everything Is Well*.............................107

Holding Tight to Reality*....................................108

Anchoring Faith..109

Life's Presence*...113

Stories From Children..115

Part V:
Yes, I Will Praise You, Lord, as the Great I AM......121

Ultimate Praise*......123

My God Ring......125

Endless Ecstasy*......127

I AM That I AM*......128

Elect*......129

I Will Praise You, Lord*......130

True Worship*......131

*Original poems

by

Janice Revels

Introduction

Power n 24/7 Praise is an eclectic writing of short stories with poems illustrating how those who read this book can have power to live victoriously throughout stress, struggles, and turmoil this life brings. This book attempts to demonstrate when including God, Jesus Christ and the Holy Spirit in daily living how praise can become habitual. Living in 24/7 praise is living with power! You will have not only power but peace, joy, love and sound mind that God provides through His word.

I invite you to wonder around in my dark closets. However, before you turn on the flashlight,

- Take a moment or two to reflect over your own life. Reflect on your current relationships, your health situations, your spiritual needs, emotional and mental circumstances. Are you where you want to be? Do you really want change for the better?
- Next, get ready for a priority shift, a paradigmatic alteration, a change in heart.
- There is no particular order in reading so you don't necessarily have to start at the beginning. Dive in anywhere with expectations to receive.
- Poem (s) following each short story will further enlighten your perception of what you just read. Be sure not to jump ahead and read them following each story.

My prayer upon completion of reading this book is that you will rethink what has become for ages an outward appearance to a perhaps inward misconception... 1). True worship is not displayed only two to three hours one day a week. 2). The power of God is not to be kept between pages of the bible, but to be put on and worn as garments of praise power!

Names are changed to protect the innocent

Power 'n' 24/7 Praise

Praise You, Lord

Lord, You blessed me, You kept me, and
You have helped me
My soul is humbled before You
Through the years of toil and pain,
my mind flashes back again and again
Where were You? *You were there!*
Tears of joy, tears of praise flow
Puddles form on the table as I sit and remember
Back to the struggles
My soul is filled with memories that humble me
Where were You? *You were there!*
Oh, how I remember — not vaguely but vividly
You were there!
Therefore have I hope, even now
as I wrap Bible after Bible
with anxious excitement,
Praying, "Lord, be with me!"
You *will* be there!
As I witness to the first of many,
planting Your seed,
Looking them in the eye,
speaking words that tell
who Jesus is, praying silently,
"Lord, give me Your words to speak!"
You *will* be there!

Part I

Will I Praise You, Lord, for All of My Days?

Back To Black?

I think not! Depressed and feeling lonely after the death of my youngest son, I realized that, even though I had been forcing myself to get out of bed, get dressed, and go to work, I'd let myself go. However, when a friend at work spoke to me about the change in my appearance, I came face to face with what was going on within me. I knew the signs of depression, because I had been there years before. I loudly voiced the same determined declaration now as I did then: "I will not allow myself to slip back to the black!" However, I couldn't do it alone. The power was not in me; otherwise, I would not have been where I was.

COMMERCIAL BREAK: If you find any help in the words of this story, if you are not a believer, but you want life, you will find yourself believing in the Gospel of Christ, as expressed in I Corinthians 15: 3-4, to become a child of God. Then let God take you from depression to confession. Confess that you believe in God and that Jesus died for you.

COMMERCIAL BREAK OVER: We will continue with the story.

I remember how what seemed the smallest thing to some was such a struggle to me. I slept with my Bible next to me, because getting up to get it took too much energy and effort. I had to read scripture, meditate, and pray again and again to digest the promises of God, which gave me the strength I needed to get out of bed. Call it what you want — "mind over matter," "a psych job," or "a crutch." Later, I found taking multi-vitamins before I went to bed was also very helpful for an early-morning energy boost. I used what worked for me to take care of being a Christian mother instead of a self-absorbed, self-pitying, buried-deep-in-a-dark-world-of-my- own-making, selfish, depressed vegetable. That is how I saw my situation. That is how I saw myself. It was all about me, me, me, and me! This depression evolved because not only did one husband reject me — but two!

The first rejection was for other women. My husband, Carlton, was 20, and I was 19. I had never been a wife before. I thought I was doing everything right. Even though I was five months pregnant when we got married, I struggled through morning sickness to cook breakfast before my husband left for work and have his dinner on the table when he came home. I thought our intimate life was great before and after the birth of our first-born. However, after about several months into our marriage, Carlton had to have *weekends* out with "the boys" (older men from his job), leaving me with sleepless nights.

After many arguments about why he had to stay out all night, he included me in his club hopping — knowing that I wouldn't enjoy it. After a month of the nightlife, I gave it up. To appease me, he opened our home to "the boys" and their significant others. I was okay with this for a while, being a perfect hostess, serving cans of beer (they poured the hard liquor themselves) and food and emptying filled ashtrays. It was better than going out. At least I did not have to pay a baby-sitter and worry about where Carlton was.

So, every other weekend, we were alone, together as a family. This lasted several months. Then, out of the blue, I was hit with accusations that it was no fun for the guys to be around a wife who only pretended that she was enjoying herself because she didn't drink, smoke, or curse — that is, everything they did. So, because he " … couldn't take it anymore …," he was going to their houses, and I could just stay home and not be bothered with smoking or cussing. Now, after almost two years of a rocky marriage, I knew Carlton, and I knew this was an excuse. I let him go.

Then, embarrassing things started happening with a female co-worker of mine who I thought was a friend. Vonda met Carlton for the first time when he came to pick me up from work a few weeks earlier. Somehow — I can't remember how — Vonda and her male friend, Shawn, Carlton, and I started going out together. One day, Vonda, who was a loud, outgoing, bold, shapely, five-foot-eight female with red tinted hair, turned the conversation in the women's lounge at work to how many ways you can please your mate. The more explicit the conversation got, the louder the laughter was from the other ladies who were there on break.

    This encouraged Vonda to be even more daring. She made it her business to direct these personal questions to me. I laughed her off, ignoring her questions by continuing to crochet. A few days later, another co-worker told me that Vonda had been messing with my husband. Apparently, Vonda had been seeing Carlton and bragging about it. I didn't believe her. But, when Carlton, infuriated, yelled at me for telling Vonda our personal business, I began to wonder what was really going on. So I asked, "Why are you talking to Vonda, anyway? For your information," I said to Carlton, "Vonda was asking questions that were none of her business. When I ignored her, she stopped. So, for her to act as if she knows what goes on in our bedroom must have been from your response to your conversation with her. Furthermore, why are you talking to her about sexual things, anyway?"

"Within the next few weeks those annoying hang up calls started not too long after that the three-day stay in isolation in the intensive care unit of the hospital was the final straw.
Mama was the one who rushed me to the emergency room after sickness sent me home early from work. I remembered being helped out of the car into the wheelchair and rolled towards the hospital doors I don't remember even going through the doors next thing I woke up 3 days later. I did not find out until after my hospital release why I was so delirious and could not walk. I guess I was not as naive as I thought considering the nights Carlton did not come home. Because of my suspicions I was too embarrassed to ask my mother. Several months later when I finally found the courage I asked, she told me about the severity of the hospital stay and the reason. I felt embarrassed

and humiliated big time, but the worst part was I felt my parents thought that *I* was the one packing the gun loaded with infectious bullets. Anger had kept me fighting in the past through each adulterous episode, but, this time, I gave up, and depression slowly started taking over.

God, along with the love I had for my three (at the time) little-girl angels, helped me keep moving. I started attending Bible studies; I involved my girls in things like choir, drum and bugle corps, girl scouts, and the bell choir. I was determined to keep my mind busy on positive things that took positive action and to permeate my mind with God's word so that I could recall scripture whenever I felt myself slipping. I would recall scriptures like, **"I can do all things through Christ which strengthens me"; "Not lagging in diligence, fervent in spirit, serving the Lord"; "God will never leave me nor forsake me" (Philippians 4:13); "There hath no temptation taken me but such as is common to man; but God is faithful, who will not suffer me to be tempted above that I am able; but will with the temptation also make a way to escape, that I may be able to bear it" (I Corinthians 10:1); and "...Greater is He that is in me than He that is in the world" (I John 4:)** just to name a few. I believe the word of God has to be in you before it can come out the instant you need it.

COMMERCIAL BREAK: It is a good time to let you know — not only did Christ die for you, but He rose again the third day,

went back to Heaven and is there now, talking with God the Father on your behalf. Why? Because He loves you in spite of what you think. You think you are too bad for God, huh? Honey, you ain't that rough and tough.

COMMERCIAL BREAK OVER: We will continue with the story.

The second rejection was for a "druggie's" life. When we first met, we talked about God and of Godly things — we were one, in one accord. So, when I found out James was a druggie, we teamed up, doubled up on prayer power. The second marriage lasted several years longer than the first not only because James lived more in state facilities than he did at home but also because I was determined not to be divorced twice. The first marriage was young, naïve love — this was real love.

Well, no matter how hard we tried, crack cocaine won. I endured being literally dragged and physically carried into drug houses, but the last straw was his drug-twisted mind thinking I would be okay in raising the daughter he always wanted. After five kids, I had my tubes tied. James was irate, so he intentionally, vengefully, impregnated another female. I felt I needed to keep my sanity and my life for myself and my children. Divorce ensued. I was now alone to raise three children (girls) by the first marriage and two additional children (boys) from the second.

Depression also ensued. I once again stepped through the one-way, black-tinted mirror doorway. I could see the bright light of hurt, suffering, and struggle of rejection on the other side, but it could not get through the doorway to harm me. The darkness was a strong force that kept the harm of light away. The blackness surrounded me. It felt so good. But I also could not feel God's love; I could not feel my children's love or give them love. So, I sat in the darkness, close to the light. It was comforting to know my God and my children's love were there, waiting for me. This made it easier to step back through the doorway into the light.

Oh, The Devil was a constant adversary. He was there to put my mind on negative cruise control, but I had learned enough from my first marriage to know that, the farther I walked into the room of darkness, the longer and harder the walk back to the light would be — the farther away, the dimmer the light. Each time, it was harder to leave the comfort of the black. How did I come out? I heaved scripture! **"Whither shall I go from thy spirit? Or whither shall I flee from thy presence? If I ascend up into heaven, thou art there: if I make my bed in hell, behold, thou art there. If I take the wings of the morning, and dwell in the uttermost parts of the sea, even there shall thy hand lead me, and thy right hand shall** hold me. If I say, 'Surely the darkness shall cover me,' even the night shall be light about me. Yea, the darkness hideth not from thee, but the night shineth as the day. The darkness and the light are both alike to thee." (Psalms 139: 7-12).** Only God kept me close to the light to bring me back through the door.

COMMERCIAL BREAK: Are you tired of the way you are living — powerless? Say no to living in sin, say no to allowing habitual sin to keep you from the peace that passes all understanding — the kind of peace that comes only from God. Will it be easy? Hell knows it can be done. That's why The Devil makes sin feel so good. Got a Bible? Read I Corinthians 10:13. If you truly believe, you will truly repent, you will truly confess, and you will truly live the life Christ gave to you by dying. For, according to the Word of God, you will truly be a child of God with the Holy Spirit to continue to help you daily.

COMMERCIAL BREAK OVER: We will continue with the story.

God and I were constant companions. I believed, I trusted, I depended on God, and He was faithful! Other Christians used to tell me to pray — with no other explanation. Just pray. Well, I am here to tell you that prayer is definitely the thing to do. However, even now, when The Devil takes my mind back to the horrible things that happened in the past, I heave up (hard and fast*)* scripture, **"Casting down imaginations and every high thing that exalteth itself against the knowledge of God and bringing into captivity every thought to the obedience of Christ." (II Corinthians 10:5).**

Then, I reach back to the verse before that to remind myself that the weapons of my warfare are not carnal, but mighty through God to the pulling down of strongholds. You must dissect the scriptures, meditate on them, and stand firm in them. Focus on the Problem Solver, not the problem. Believe that the Spirit exists in you and gives you power to overcome; then pray with all your spirit, according to the word of God. Believe in the power of God. What you are doing is building that fantastically intimate relationship with your Heavenly Father. You are building strength to fight the good fight of faith to win whatever the battle is that you are going through.

My children are now grown, with children of their own. Now, years later, The Devil still tries to use the same tactics to get me back to the black. As soon as hurt arises, like the death of my son, that old Devil reminds me of how safe a place depression is, away from the hurts of the world. Depression is sneaky. It can lure you to the doorway by making you feel you are all alone in a roomful of people and that none of them cares anything about you.

But, God sends you reminders. In my case, the reminder was in the form of a friend saying, "Hey, what's going on with you?" This reminder says that you *are* thought about. **"How precious also are thy thoughts unto me, O God! How great is the sum of them! If I should count them, they are more in number than the sand: When I awake, I am still with thee." (Psalms 139: 17-18).** You cannot even imagine it: The Sovereign God, Creator of infinity, Creator of the universe and everything in it, has His mind on you so much that you cannot begin to wrap your brain around it. God is the Infinite Lover that will rock your world and hold your existence in His loving hands. So, with boldness, you can just let the Devil know that, by the power Christ Jesus has invested in you, he has lost the stronghold of depression he had you chained with. You can loudly voice the same determined declaration now as I did then: "I will not allow myself to slip back to the black!" Then shout, "GLORY TO GOD!"

SIDENOTE

1/**3**/73 — my oldest girl was born.
3/6/7**6** — my second girl was born.
6/8/7**8** — my third daughter was born.

I may never know the real reason for this **numerical** pattern — where the number that ends the year preceding is the same as the number of the month of the next birth, and the date of the month on which the birth occurred is the same as the last digit of the year of that birth. But I know such patterns and happenings have occurred throughout my life. All of these occurrences solidify the knowledge that God is in control and has a special plan for my life.

The Silent Destroyer
versus
The Great Restorer

I lay on the couch where I flopped
After an eight-hour workday.
My girls, who were twelve, nine, and seven,
asked, "What's for dinner?"
I heard my voice talking,
through the growing fog,
Telling them to be careful with the hot stove.
What was for dinner? I didn't know.
I had already slipped into a grayish sludge.
I had no more energy. I had no more strength.
Please, God, watch over my children.
I woke three hours later
to a dinner plate left on the stove
And a semi-clean kitchen.
I ate, washed the rest of the dishes,
Turned out the kitchen light
With tears now dropping harder from my eyes.
I cried out in shame and despair.
I declared, "No more! No more! No more!
I can do all things through Christ,
which strengthens me!"
I pulled the covers over my girls,
Knelt beside their beds, and prayed,
"Dear God, this has become a ritual,
With my girls taking care of themselves *and* me.
Please give me the strength to come out of myself,
out of this Self-pitying state of hopelessness.
If it is true that, 'Greater is He that is in me than
he that is in the world,'
Then I am not raising my children alone
Any longer! I am calling You on your promise:
Here we are Lord —
What is Your future for us?"

How Bright, the Dark, Cloudy Days

As clouds move shadows across hills and valleys,
Shadows move across the face of my life,
Giving the appearance of dread and gloom
When hope is caught between
the shadowy days of uncertainty
And brief glimpses of flickering light.
Rays of light puncture
as a needle pricks gray clouds,
And darkness slowly diminishes in density, and
Illumination — ever so slowly — dissipates the
grayish mass.
Shifting shadows slowly, but steadily,
alter more hills than valleys.
The gift of shadows is the
thankfulness and beauty of light.
LIGHT reigns!
Blessed be God, the Light of life!

Youthful Encounter

Oh, he was cool in his narrow shades and brownish crew-cut hairstyle. He was tall and lanky — and just my type. It did not matter that he stuttered a little. He was interested in me, the shy, inexperienced seventeen-year-old girl with the boney, shapeless legs. I was with my two brothers, who were meeting up with Frank's sister Candice. Candice was an outgoing, outspoken, good-humored 21-year-old busty female who wore short skirts and tight-fitting blouses. My brother, who was 19, had been dating Candice for three weeks. They did not tell me then, but they planned for me to meet Candice's younger brother. I'd never been on a blind date — good thing it worked out well.

My other brother's girlfriend was already at the house party. We did just that — partied all night long. Frank and I dated. We did what normal teenagers did. We went to movies, house parties (which was the thing at the time), and bowling. We had been dating for a few months, when, one evening, sitting in my house watching television, Frank gave me a promise ring. The little diamond was just that — little. Nevertheless, I loved it and all that it stood for: My promise to him and his promise to me to be special friends, to be together and see if we could develop our special friendship into love. Everyone knows that, after the promise ring comes the engagement ring and that, after that, comes the wedding ring. After all, we were of age to think about marriage.

The next weekend, we went out and had an exceptionally good time. We made out in the back seat of Frank's two-door, dark-green Ford. We enjoyed the drive-in movies between kissing and petting. We only petted on top of our clothes. I was a good girl. When we got to my house after the movies, even though it was late, he came in. When we got to the kitchen, Frank asked for some water. Frank followed me to the sink. I ran the cold tap water. I asked him if he wanted ice. When he did not answer, I turned around. He had his signature Frank Piper grin, with all his

Uh-Uh! No way!

How many times must I say?
You don't even have to ask that question again
We live in an apathetic world full of sin
Living in a world of chaos
Rampant crimes of murder, child abuse,
Wars, rumors of wars, with no sign of truce
Starvation, terrorist bombings,
Hijackings,
Uh-uh! No way!
Ain't going to happen!
How many times must I say?
To Live without my God, my Savior,
my Refuge in these Days
Uh-uh! Absolutely no way!

Part III

Will I Praise You, Lord, for Blessings From Above?

pearly whites showing. I went to dreamland. "Oh, this has to be love," I thought.

As I stared at him in a daze, I noticed his shoulders gently flinched, which made me look away from his dreamy smile to his hands. I immediately snapped out of the dream state and gasped in innocence. I actually felt the blood, fluid — whatever drains from your face — draining from mine from sheer embarrassment and horror. My mind raced. Yes, we had had a good time! Yes, we had been a little more intimate than we should have been, but why would he think it was time for this gigantic step? Why would he think it was okay to reveal himself to me like that? He did not just let it dangle, but he was moving it back and forth as in anticipated triumph — with that darn grin on his face! And right in my parents' kitchen!

I had seen on television the night before where the girl slapped the guy — it was justified. I thought this was a good time for me to do the same. Feeling every bit justified, I slapped Frank right across his jaw. However, what happened next did not happen the same way as on the television show. Frank slapped me back. "O-M-G!" or, as we said back then, "H E double hockey sticks!" I lit into him like he was a firecracker ready to be popped on the 4th of July. We traded blows. He skirted one off the side of my head, but I solidly landed several. No way was he going to act like the chip off the old block with me. I secretly knew Frank's father abused his mother.

One day, Candice had been crying. She confided in me — without telling me straight out — but she said enough for me to know and to know it happened on a regular basis. Frank's father was short and heavy, and his mother was short and very petite. They seemed to be a happy couple. If I had not lived in somewhat the same situation, I would have thought Candice was exaggerating. Why do men feel a necessity to beat on women? They are supposed to be men who cherish and love their wives as Christ loves the church. A man is supposed to treat his wife as if she were his own flesh. This is what God himself commands and expects.

Because I knew of the abuse in Frank's family, I needed Frank never to forget what hitting *me* meant. I was fighting for his mother, for my mother, and for all the abused females in the world! I became crazed! Frank wrenched out of my grip. I stood there, looking at the scratches on his face and neck turning red. *Oh yes,* I thought, *he will be nursing himself for about a week or even longer,* because one of the scratches was deep enough to have drawn blood. I felt the side of my head throbbing. I was too angry to feel the slap on my cheek but knew I would in the morning. *Oh no! I will not be going through this!* I cared about Frank, but I had a choice, and I prayed to God that I would always have a choice and not choose to be in an abusive relationship.

I took off the dinky promise ring and threw it as hard as I could in the trashcan and yelled, "Get out!" Frank picked up the trashcan and turned it over, emptying the contents all over the kitchen floor. He hurriedly skimmed through the scattered mess, looking for the ring. He did not find it. He looked at me like he was going to ask for help finding it. I yelled, "Don't even think about it — just get out"! I guess he saw I was heating up for another round. He picked up his sunglasses from the floor where I had slapped them off his face. He was puffing hard from exhaustion and anger. However, he didn't say a word. He just glared at me, turned, and, letting the screen door slam behind him, he was gone.

I was boiling, too mad to cry, too hot to simmer. I paced the floor, trying to calm down. Then I wondered why my parents did not come down from their bedroom. There was no way they hadn't heard all the noise. Even if they were sleep, I'm sure we woke them. I quickly dropped to my knees to pick up the trash spread across the floor before they — especially Dad — came downstairs. I swooped up an armload of trash, not bothering to look for the ring. When the trash was taken out the next morning, I did not even blink. *Let it burn,* I thought. Ten minutes later, my youngest brother, eight, came in with the ring, showing everybody and saying Frank owes him five dollars. I left the room, not wanting to talk about the humiliating episode.

I did not see or talk to Frank until years later. I was picking up my 14- and 13-year-old boys from a basketball tournament. I ran in just to let them know I was there. My hair was half-combed, I was looking rough, and I did not really care that I had put on 40 pounds over the past several years. I was overweight and looked a mess. Did I say I didn't care? However, when I literally bumped into Frank, I was excruciatingly aware of my shabby attire — faded jeans and sweatshirt, with dirty, worn-out tennis shoes. I don't think I had even brushed my teeth.

Frank, as usual, was "dressed to impress," wearing a three-piece jogging suit with matching shoes. He was as surprised to see me as I was to see him. He did not seem to notice my appearance. He was talking fast but barely stuttering. However, one thing that always amazed me about him was that he seemed to take in the whole picture at one glance. He had a sharp eye for details and a good memory. I could tell he was excited to see me. In the brief conversation, he asked me if I lived in the same house on Circle Drive. I said, "Yes" and asked him how he knew where I lived.

He explained that, one day, Candice, who knew where I lived through my brother, showed him the house as they happened to pass by. I asked him about the young boy with him. He stated it was his son, but that he and the mother were divorced. I told him I was separated. My sons ran up to us with questioning expressions on their faces that demanded an answer. "Who is this man?" Without waiting for them to verbalize their question with tones that matched their facial inquiries, I introduced them to Frank, who commented on their good games. Frank and I said our good-byes.

Over the next few years, I had occasional thoughts of Frank and how we never had closure to our relationship that ended so abruptly. Perhaps one day we will. Then, several months

Will I Praise You, Lord, for All My Days?

later, one evening, there was a knock on the door. It was Frank. I was not expecting him but was glad to see him. My children were doing homework. I had a rule that, if and when I ever dated, I would not invite any man to my house unless I knew we would marry. I valued the spiritual foundation I was laying for my children, and my intentions were not to confuse them.

So, I stepped out in the cool of the early evening to talk to Frank on the front porch. I was glad it was not late and dark. Frank and I talked briefly about his past marriage and my present separation. I asked about Candice and his parents. It was a good conversation, and I enjoyed the visit. We said good-bye, and we said we would stay in touch; we kissed. I thought it would be a light, brief peck on the lips, a friendly gesture of good-bye for now and that this little smooch would, hopefully, encourage him to call me. These were my intentions.

However, Frank grabbed hold of me like a leech. Now, I was the one trying to get away. I was upset with myself for allowing that kiss to happen. It was just that, while we were talking, I once again went to dreamland, thinking, *Why not start the relationship again, since we still like each other?* Wow! Now, suddenly, the dream had become a nightmare! I was so disappointed and gosh-darn mad! We had not seen each other for several months, and before that, we had had a 10-minute encounter in the midst of a very busy basketball tournament. Before that, it had been years since our abrupt departure as "special friends." What in the world made him think he could tongue-lash me into a sexual relationship? His tongue hit every tooth and molar in my mouth like a ball bouncing off pegs in a pinball machine. I thought that, if I bit down, I would taste his blood before he let me go. So, I decided to groin him. Lucky for him, he stopped the second I had made my decision. Once again, he was leaving mad. And why in the world would he be mad? Okay: Clearly, this man has issues. I thought, *This is not the closure I wanted but definitely what I need to stamp this used-to-be, want-to-be relationship CLOSED!*

Seeing Frank again brought back memories. I could not keep my mind from going back to my previous relationships. My first husband hit me once — and it was not that I did not forgive him for that. After he laid his open palm across my face, I made it vividly clear that, if he ever hit me again, he was not going to wake up the same. He never hit me again. I learned a lesson from that slap — not to provoke. Even though we were in an intense argument, someone had to be in control. Why risk getting hurt by getting all up in your man's face — egging him on with hellish talk? He intended to hurt me, and he did — not only physically but emotionally as well.

My second husband slapped me once as well. He was high on drugs and on his way out the door. I was sitting on the couch with my children. I had learned not to argue while he was in this stupor. I had already braced myself for the blow. He had never hit me before, but, somehow, I knew he was going to. I felt the blow, but I guess that, because I had stiffened my jaw, the slap stung for only a few seconds. He kept walking — not stopping to look back or say anything. Even in his stupor, he would not chance staying after that. I am not all big and bad, but I do believe that I am better than being someone's punching bag. After all, I know God loves me unconditionally.

I often visit the scriptures that tell me who I am in Christ. Christ has me sold on believing I am special, too special to allow anyone to beat on me and damage my spirit, my emotions, and the physical temple that God has given me. I am learning to take care of myself. I have fixed the problem of thinking, "I don't care." I now care about how I look and who I am. Perhaps that is why Frank thought he could treat me as he did: I projected a lack of self-confidence. Never again! I found it in God. I invite you to do the same.

Abuse on the Outside Looking In

A little girl seeing
the slap of a big heavy hand
on the face of a loving mother,
hearing her screams and cries,
seeing the tears in her eye,
seeing mother sprawled on the
floor, pulled up by her hair,
only to be slapped down again.
Learning to cringe at the
first sound
of every word said loudly
knowing what will follow and
wanting to run and hide.
But staying to yell, "Stop!"
could make a difference
between a few slaps or a beating.
Hearing the yelling, cussing and fussing,
sitting close by, scared and trembling,
crying and screaming within
but ready to defend —
even if it meant being beaten again.

Part II

Will I Praise You, Lord, for Keeping Me in Your Way?

Not Always Pure and Righteous

Early morning on "D-Day," I emerged from underneath the white and lavender ruffled lace bedspread to see unsoiled layers of newspaper. I pulled the spread back over me and buried my sobs of uncontrollable despair in the pillow. The realization that the days of "Red-rover, red-rover, send Needa right over" were forever gone brought deeper sobs. Even though I was 19, on occasion, I would join the younger generation in the middle of the street to play the fun childhood game. I went over in my mind for the hundredth time the events of the past months.

So the ladies at work were right. They knew what I didn't know until now. To them, all the sleeping at my desk at work was an unmistakable, telltale sign. I was so embarrassed to suddenly jerk awake to find my supervisor glaring down at me. It seemed no matter how early I went to bed, before mid-day I was nodding off into a deep sleep. When it happened the third time, Mrs. Kelly called me to her desk and asked me some candid and embarrassing questions that made me face reality. I would no longer be looked upon as innocent. At that moment, I still didn't know the full reality. Was I that naïve?

Then there was the time, at Sears, that my sister, Karen, and I walked the 3½ blocks to the clothing store. When we arrived on that Saturday morning, the store was crowded. We went to the catalogue section. Back then, you ordered by phone, and then, a few days later, you'd go to the store to pick your item up. I picked up our number, and we waited for the clerk to call it to get our items. It seemed the longer I stood, the sicker I got. I looked from face to face trying to see if anyone would have pity on me. I was too scared to ask anyone for help or ask anyone if they would let me sit down for just a minute.

I walked, in slow motion, around a small area, looking for an empty seat. I know people knew something was wrong with me, because they kept staring at me as if they wanted to ask me, "What in the world is wrong with you?" In spite of my looking sick, no one came to my aid or moved from their seat. Finally, out of desperation, since I thought I would pass out, I spotted a space between chairs where no one was standing. I flew to that empty space, knelt, and upchucked with such force and sound that everything that was in me came out, splattering against the baseboard and floor. You had better believe, people moved out of their seats then. When I looked up, the seats on either side of me were empty; everyone was standing and staring. Even then, I thought I was coming down with the flu; I didn't connect any of the things that had happened within the past month with any other possibility.

This morning should have been the beginning of the monthly torment that I normally hated. I should have awakened to crimson-colored sheets. My period usually happens while I am sleeping, so I had learned to place newspaper under my lower body at night. My body worked like a time clock every month; however, this was the third month in a row that I was a "no show."

I couldn't talk to God. In fact, I had been hiding from God ever since that day in the basement with my boyfriend. We had been careful with the heavy petting and the timely extractions — but not on that particular day. I remember pushing and him pulling, not letting go, me saying, "No," — but too late. I hoped — but didn't pray (because I knew I had sinned) that the first time would not make me pregnant. I was too ashamed to ask, "Why, God?" I know why — all my younger life, I had heard the older women say, "You play with fire, you get burned." I didn't know then if that was in the Bible, but I knew the scripture that said, "What's done in secret will come to light" (Luke 8:17; Matthew 10:24-27; and Luke 12:1-3).

Whenever under my mother's watchful eye, I tried to act my old self through the undeniable changes of pregnancy. I don't know how long it was before my parents found out. I normally was quiet and stayed in my room, reading books, so I didn't have to pretend around them much. I did not have a clue they knew until I was called to the dining room. I walked slowly down the stairs — scared. I remember all three of us standing and my mother telling one of my siblings, as he walked into the room, to leave.

Oh, my mother's tone let me know something was coming, and "my condition" was the only thing different. I wanted to say, "God, help me," but I didn't want to bring God into my sinful mess. I felt utterly alone. Dad was mad. Mom was upset but nurturing. "Marriage" was the key and constantly recurring word. My unaware, soon-to-be husband and his mother and older, married-with-kids sister were summoned. My mind continued bringing up the scripture about being unequally yoked. I knew the baby's father was not a committed believer. But who was I to judge that he would never be?

By my fifth month of pregnancy, Carlton and I were standing in front of the assistant preacher — because pastors were too righteous to marry anyone who committed such sin (despite my faithful participation in church). That realization made we think of all the lives I had touched in a negative way by my few minutes of lustful desire. Even though we had put furniture in layaway before having sex, this young man of 20 still had the option — as did I — to change his mind about marrying. However, now, there seemed to be no other way. My parents and his family would not have had to suffer any anxiety because of our sin. The person marrying us would not have to redirect his busy schedule to take the time to do what my beloved pastor wanted to do but now couldn't.

In August of 1972, I married. Oh, I loved Carlton. I didn't completely blame him — or at least not as much as I blamed myself. However, when my husband decided he did not want to be married — which was probably the day after the wedding, although he didn't verbalize it until a few months after — signs of his unfaithfulness became apparent. It didn't seem to matter that I was his wife and pregnant. This cut me to the core.

Months passed. I could not take it anymore. I knew what I had to do —get a butcher knife and a plan. Well, the thought definitely came to mind, but no. I had to make amends with God. I knew I could not get through this anguish without Him — though I tried. The almost-two years I had isolated myself from God made me dry and parched. I wanted to drink Him in slowly — does that make any sense? In other words, I think what I was doing was crawling back, trying to get some Godliness inside before facing God head-on. I picked up Helen Steiner Rice and *Apples of Gold* to moisten and ready my soul. Then I read Psalms and Proverbs to further prepare my heart for the shower that I knew was coming.

All this, of course, directed me to God, but I had to show God that I loved Him and wanted Him in my life. It was all about shame. Shame for what I had done and then more shame for not respecting Him as my Father to tell all my troubles to. I was ashamed for not having faith to believe He could and would handle the mess I had made of myself. Then more shame descended on me for thinking that I had any other recourse but Him. I bowed humbly before Him. Because of who He is, it didn't take long to be back in my Father's loving arms — and just in time.

You know all the things some marriages go through in the early stages — infidelity, staying out late hours of the night, and, then, the late nights turn into early-morning arrivals. I remembered once packing my toddler in the car seat about 11:00 at night, driving around in unknown neighborhoods, thinking I would see his car. I got lost. What in God's name was I doing? Oh, foolish one of little faith. When I finally found my way back to familiar territory, I vowed I would never do such a stupid thing again to risk the safety of my daughter and myself getting lost late in the dark night somewhere in never-seen-before-and-will-never-see-again land. When I finally arrived home at 1:30 in the morning, guess who wasn't there? What I did and should have been doing all along was to read every scripture on marriage — and not just read, but *study*. If I could so easily lose sight of God,

I needed more of His word in me.

In the months to come, hang-up calls started all times of night. One night, the calls continued after midnight, about every 10 minutes. Out of frustration, I answered sweetly, "Listen, honey, my husband is not here. I am nine months pregnant and need all the rest I can get. So, whatever time he does come home, I promise, I will have him call you. So, can you please stop calling?" There was a pause, but I waited; then, the female voice said, "Okay," and hung up. Upon my husband's mid-day arrival, I informed him of the call and asked him to please, please, please call her. He stared at me dumbfounded. I guess he saw the seriousness on my face and figured he'd better do it right then. I heard him talking to her on the phone. I didn't try to listen — it really didn't matter. The conversation did not go very well. Apparently, I had given her too much information — the lie he was living with her caught up with him. He tried to take his frustration out on me, but it wasn't happening.

SIDENOTE: One time, a sister in the Lord told me that the Spirit of God and the spirit of The Devil cannot live in the same space. I held tight to that and actually made that my warrior's theme, along with many other scriptures. However, I had to read this in the Bible myself. I mean, it sounded logical, but was it scriptural? So I researched it and found many, many supporting scriptures and whole chapters, such as: Romans 8; Galatians 5:16-17; James 1: 11-18; and practically the whole New Testament.

In light of this new information, I became the sweetest wife ever. How? My focus switched. I made a new resolution: This devil working in Carlton was either going to leave his body and convert to the control of the Holy Spirit of God or pack up and leave with his body, devilish spirit and all. Now, it was war! I clung to II Corinthians 10:4-6. I studied more, went to church and Bible study more, and even had Bible studies in my home. I committed scriptures to memory and application. My charge: Change my home to complete compliance with the Spirit of God, forcing all demonic spirits to leave. One study led me to another, and, before long, I was enjoying the word of God and living it with peace and joy. There was little change in my husband but a big change in me. I guess he could not take it anymore. He moved out. Do you think I felt victorious in Jesus?

One day, I answered the telephone, and the voice gave her name. It was the same name I heard my husband use about a year or so earlier. The voice explained that she lived out of state in the city where she and my husband had lived and met before he moved to Kansas City. They continued their relationship by telephone calls and letters. Sylvia was not aware that he was married and certainly did not know we were having a baby. Hurt by his betrayal, she severed their relationship. She said, just a few months after that, he called her and told her we were having marital problems and that he had left. Therefore, they started back talking, But now, as before, he only calls her occasionally. By this time, she was crying and saying she did not know what to do, since she lived so far away. I informed her that God don't like ugly and you reap what you sow. I gave Sylvia more news: Not only is he married, but this is his third child by me. On top of that, I told her that, most likely, he was out doing to her with someone else what he and she did to me. I probably should have resisted saying some of that. Perhaps something in my voice prompted her to continue talking, apologizing for the calls, and the whole nine yards. I said to myself, "Why, God is this home wrecker crying to me?" Well, why did I direct that question to God? God answered, "We (Christians) are the light of the world ... a light not hidden under a bushel" (Matthew 5:15). My heart was touched. I felt my Christian duty was to administer godly love and forgiveness. My tone and attitude changed, and I began to minister to her. I could do this because my spirit was not chained to a failed marriage. God had nurtured me through, and I had given my marriage all that was required of me to give as a Christian wife. On July 7, 1978, I filed for divorce.

I look back to see how God was so intimate in my life and how His loving arms gave me strength to love the unlovable. I was not mean and evil toward my husband, even while he was doing everything to get me and the kids out of the house so he could live there with his other woman (he told me this years later).

I faced possible eviction, a serious hospital stay in which I was comatose for three days, in isolation, because of his infidelity, and was subject to humiliation and embarrassment with family and friends. I held on to God's promises in his word. God brought me through the stress and anguish of raising three children on one income while reclaiming my house.

God showed up mightily in my life after I finally understood that I could not do it myself. I tried so hard to swim but could only barely tread water. I felt a constant dipping under and coming back up choking, with nose and mouth full of water, gasping for air, and kicking and flapping for life. It was awful without God. But because of God's favor on my life, He did not let me sink (God never left me). Instead, I learned how to swim. Now I know for sure that, with God, I can make it through any vortex in life. God's grace and mercy kept me.

My second marriage happened eight years later. This time, my parents said, "Don't marry!" I married. The marriage lasted a little longer than the first — 10 years. I ended up raising five children on the same single-parent income. I was grateful for the life lessons God had taught that had brought me through my past turbulence and into a closer relationship with Him — because this second marriage was to be a massive whirlpool! *What is true worship?*

Reaping the Consequence...

...sown way back when
once young, innocent, and full of lust
letting a fine, handsome thing win my trust
pregnant before wedding
not once but twice
choosing to ignore the loving Godly advice
to keep what is chaste and pure holy
to concentrate on giving myself fully
to the One Who will never leave me alone
or break the promise to be there lifelong.
Reaping the consequences of sin,
struggling with singleness,
seeing no light at the end
longing for a God-sent spouse to share
my life, my secrets, my most sincere prayer.
Now, years later,
I am still without marriage, maybe.
But there is doubt
nevertheless, a sure lesson learned.
Walk in the spirit, and you will not burn.

Old Days, New Ways

Do you remember Paul and how he spoke boldly to the Galatian Christians about mixing the law with their newfound Christianity? He admonished those among them who would pervert the gospel. I know people like the Galatian Christians who supposedly are Christians but believe bad luck will follow if they split poles, put their purses on the floor, break mirrors, or walk under ladders, and Christians who believe the saying, "If I didn't have bad luck, I'd have no at all." Do you believe that believing in luck and fate goes against the Christian faith that teaches God is in ultimate control as the Creator of everything?

Step on a crack, break your mother's back. I don't know which of my five children spoke that into existence, but I have been suffering with back problems for the past 13 years. LOL! If I believed in such nonsense, I would be dead or literally crazy by now. If I believed fate is in control, I could not believe the scripture in James 1:17 that says, *"Every good and perfect gift comes from above."* I am the one who breaks those time-consuming email chains, the ones that say, "Send to seven to ten people within 30 minutes, and you will have a sudden flow of money within the next three days" or "Pray this prayer, and you will receive a blessing." You might as well play the lottery or spend your evenings and nights pulling the arm down on the slot machines.

Superstitious belief and sayings have been part of every generation, manifesting throughout the years in different forms. Satan's tactics have not changed since the Garden of Eden because he knows they work — subtle, crafty, and cunning are a few adjectives used in the various Biblical translations that describe him. Satan has modernized the old superstitious myths to fate that comes via emails and crafty ways of working them into the family. He will do anything to take your mind off God. For instance, if the bride steps on the threshold as she enters her new home, this will bring the worst of luck to the marriage; thus the tradition developed that the husband sweeps the blushing bride into his arms to carry her over the threshold. Then there is the superstition that, if the groom drops the ring during the ceremony, the marriage is doomed — thus, the best man hands the ring to the groom. Why believe in anything different? Tradition is good even if its origin is superstitious. It's harmless ... or is it?

Is it really a myth that if you lived together before marriage, your marriage will last? That is the actual reason given by some unmarried people who live together. According to the old *and* new ways, my parents should have divorced years ago. Why hold on to a marriage "just for the kids"? "Live and let live." My parents recently celebrated their 60th wedding anniversary. It was hard getting pictures of them together. I found pictures with both of them, but they were not sitting or standing close together. I gathered more pictures from my siblings that showed our parents sitting closer, but not smiling. Looking through the pictures with the person who was to use the best picture on their anniversary invitation, she jokingly said, "Do your parents like each other"? This remark hit hard. This remark sent my mind swirling back to childhood.

My siblings and I grew up in a loving home. Then, as the years went by, our home was happier when both parents were not there. Most of the time, Mother was in the home cooking and working (she had a home business). When Dad came home, he would not stand for a piece of paper on the hand waxed to a shine linoleum floor or dust on the polished-to-mirror-perfection end tables. When Dad came home from work, kids scattered, disappearing until he called for us. For some reason, I considered our family typical — two parents and six kids. Back then, many families consisted of two parents and up to 12 or 14 kids. I remember, as a child, walking outside after dinner. Sometimes, as I walked up and down the sidewalk, trying to decide which playmate's door to knock on, I heard yelling coming through the open doors. I distinctly remember one time going home after hearing yelling from three different friends' houses. There was plenty of yelling in our house, too. As a kid, I wanted to make up a new superstition: If you yelled too loud, your inner eardrum would burst. Maybe people would honor this superstition as much as they did others, making homes more peaceful. Of course, being so young, it wasn't for me to understand the stress of parents providing for their families. I just knew my daddy worked hard, leaving early every morning.

One day, not too long ago, my sister shared with me a delicate, touching moment — one that is rare for us to see or hear of. This was my parents speaking sweetly to each other. "Clifford, will you do this (whatever it was) for me?" Then Dad, without a fuss or question, went straightway and did it. When he returned, he said, "Angie, I did (such and such). Is that the way you wanted it done?" Angie would say, "Yes, that is exactly the way I wanted it — thank you." You might think this is a simple conversation — no big deal. However, coming from my parents, well, let's just say Karen thought it was amazing enough to tell me about it with excitement.

Some may have looked at my parents' marriage and deemed it unsalvageable. Of all the reasons that couples stay together after years of marriage, can anyone other than the couple say it is only because of convenience and complacency? I still remember the little smooches and pats on the butt between my parents. I remember the good times as well as the bad times. I remember the entire family going to the peach and apple orchards, picking the ripe, juicy fruits by the bushels or stopping at a roadside fruit stand when traveling. I remember my parents sitting together, talking, while peeling all that fruit, paring knives working hard and fast, Mom stirring large pots on the stove, Dad helping her get them off when done, and the house smelling so good with bubbling sweet preserves, jams and jellies. WOW! All of this happening with Dad and Mom working hard together, as a team.

Even today, 60-plus years later, my parents sit in their individual recliners in front of the large flat-screen to enjoy the same picture. Over the years, they have acquired a mutual taste for each other's television programs, as they made compromises. Now, *Mom* talks about sports, and *Dad* watches soap operas and religious channels! It's *still* a mutual sharing and a team effort. I look at my parents after what seems like a lifetime of bitter sweets (as a child, it seemed like more bitter than sweet) and say, "Don't bring to me anything about fate and superstition — giving up on marriage because of what an outsider (or even the children) think they see and know. Even though we kids were in the home, we were not there at the beginning when the courtship started, when the google-eyes were bright and beaming. We don't know the details about how the foundation for their marriage was laid. For instance, Dad met Mom, who was a preacher's kid, and started going with Mom to church. Dad's religious background was being baptized in a small creek in Sandy County, Texas as a Methodist when he was thirteen. Dad was baptized again in the same church that Mom grew up in, and they got married there. We were born, and our parents continued going there as a family most Sundays. They have a commonality. We can't change the plan that God has for them — which fate has nothing to do with. Just to let you know, Daddy did not carry Mom over the threshold! I don't know if Mom wore "old, new, borrowed or blue and a penny in her shoe," which are supposed to bring luck to the bride. Cans were not tied to the back of their car (the tying of metal cans behind a newlywed couple's car is another version of the superstition that metal protects and brings wealth). I do know that, whereas fate, luck, and superstition proceed from chance; favor, blessing, and grace flow from God without restraint if you are a child of God. Does being a child of God make it wrong to believe in the old traditions of the world?

    Please, don't misunderstand. I am sure there are old ways I still cling to. Some may be so deeply rooted within that I don't think of them as old ways: If I continue to cut my hair, will there come a time when it will not grow back? If I don't believe I have talent, will I not succeed in anything, no matter how hard I try? My prayer is that we will learn from the old ways. Even though games of chance and superstitions are prevalent today, it is still a subtle form of casting your vote toward fate instead of God.

When I see a penny on the ground, I don't look to see if it is face side up or tail side up (face side up is supposed to bring luck). Rather, as I bend down to pick it up, I say loudly, "Thank you, God, for the money."

Allow your faith in God to enable you to discard all the old superstitions and bring you into a new way, a better day, of trusting God to supply all your needs. You just might find yourself committed to a 60-plus-year relationship with God because you are now realizing what "true worship" really is.

A New Life in Christ

How faithful You are every day
To wake me each morning to newness of life
I'm so thankful for Your grace
You made available to all
Though few will answer the call
I heard your message, believed, and repented.
Oh, this new life isn't easy
When I try to
Put down what the Bible says is sleazy
But the love You gave me through the
Death of Your son
Has me feeling
So very special and strong enough to overcome.
How faithful You are every day
To wake me each morning to live life Your way.

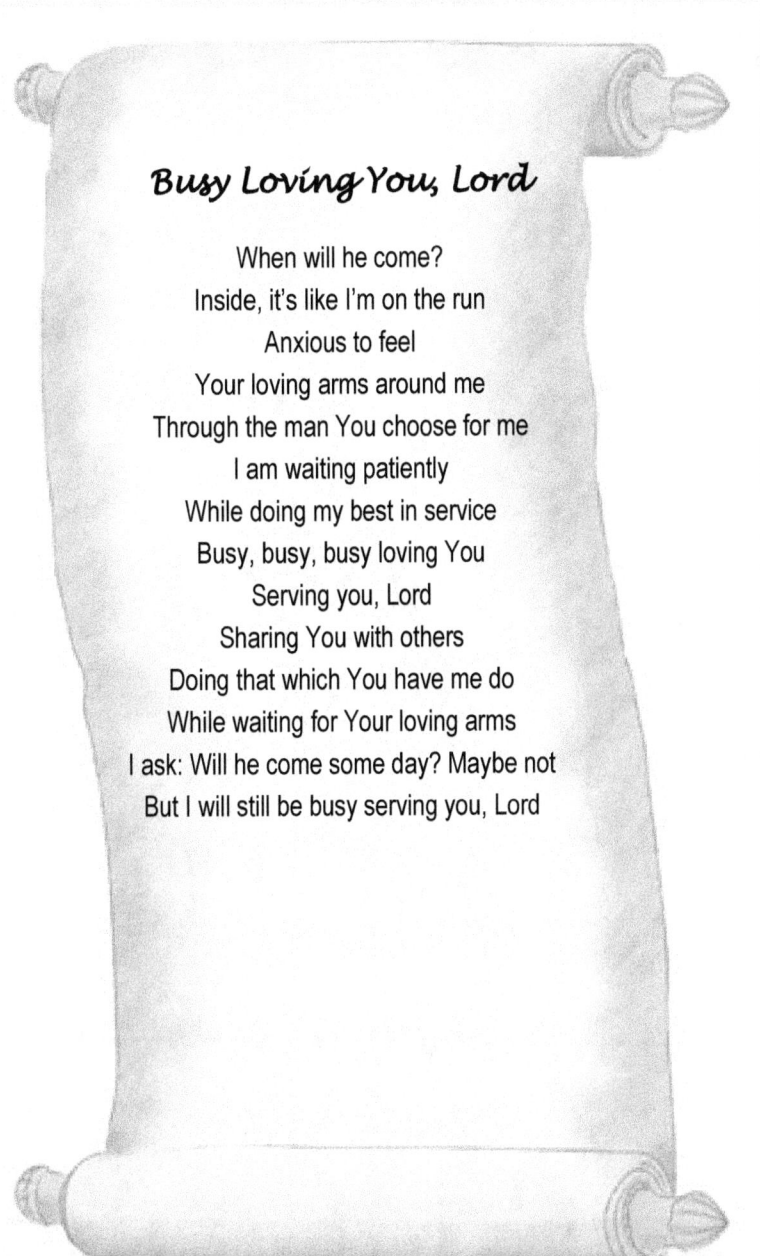

Busy Loving You, Lord

When will he come?
Inside, it's like I'm on the run
Anxious to feel
Your loving arms around me
Through the man You choose for me
I am waiting patiently
While doing my best in service
Busy, busy, busy loving You
Serving you, Lord
Sharing You with others
Doing that which You have me do
While waiting for Your loving arms
I ask: Will he come some day? Maybe not
But I will still be busy serving you, Lord

Crazy Chimes

The doorbell rang. Up I jumped at 8:30 p.m. from sleeping on the couch in front of the TV. It was not quite dark when I looked through the big window to see who was ringing the doorbell. I saw no one. As I turned away, the bell sounded again. I yelled, "Who is it?" No one responded. This time, I went and looked out the door window. The low door window allowed me to see the full porch. No one was there. As I was looking out the window, the bell rang again. *Okay, why is the little boy who lives down the street playing games?* I thought. I ran to the window in the back of the house, threw the window up, and shot my head out ready to fire off some choice words, but no one was ringing the back door bell.

When the box was installed, I requested the chimes be different to distinguish the front from the back door. For some reason, it did not happen. As I raced back to the front of the house, I was determined to catch the little booger. I quickly ran to the front, but I saw no one.

I stopped. I was tired. *This is ridiculous!* I thought. *Here I am, running back and forth. What I need to do is think logically. It is dark now. Even if the side gate to the back yard was unlocked, who would go to the back at night to ring the doorbell? Okay — there is a logical answer to this logical question. Khloe'! Has the dog learned to ring the doorbell?* I was serious!

Then I laughed, "Don't be silly, girl. Who would take the time to train a dog to ring the doorbell — and for what purpose?" Well, then *what?* I put my hands on my hips and sternly said, "Ricky, are you ringing the doorbell?" The same eerie feeling came over me as it did the first night I was alone with Ricky's urn. That is even sillier, since the Bible says, "Once dead — the judgment." Ricky's spirit is in Heaven — not ringing my doorbell.

The next day, my daughter-in-law was home when the

doorbell rang. I went to the door — there was no one there. By now, this was the third time this had happened. The bell chimed again. I watched my daughter look out the door. No one was there. She looked at me in puzzlement. I told her with a serious look on my face, "It's Ricky ringing the doorbell." She was on her way to look out the same back window that I had looked out several times, and, on her way, she said, "Is it Khloe'?" She turned to me and smiled as if to say, "Which is crazier — to believe a dog was ringing the bell or a spirit?"

All this happened three days ago. Just now as I am closing this short story, the doorbell rings. It took me only two seconds to get to the door, since the computer is about 10 steps away. My oldest son asked who was at the door. I said, "It's just Ricky, playing games again." My son, Rusty, grinned. The weird thing about it is that Khloe' barks just before the bell rings — just as she does when someone actually comes into the yard. Weird?

Will I Praise You, Lord, for Blessings From Above?

Searched and Found

I was happy to tag along with my mother everywhere she went. I was a momma's girl. I had so much love and respect for my Mom. It seems I have loved the Lord all my life, I guess, because my mother did. I went with momma everywhere — to all the church functions that were held at our home church and all over the city and in other cities. I loved to travel on the church bus to everywhere the choir had to sing. I think I inherited being a Christian through osmosis. I listened to every word preached wherever we went. I enjoyed the old songs and spiritual hymns that had so much to say about the love of God and the love we should have for Him.

As I grew older, in my teenage years, I started noticing the difference in what was being preached from one minister to the next. Sunday morning church service was "worship as usual." Did they not decide just last Sunday, on this very subject, that the Bible taught that, once you were baptized, you didn't need to be baptized a second time and once saved, always saved? I didn't know hardly anything at the age of 18, but I would think that God would not make it so hard for man to know what He was saying in the Bible. I shook my head even harder when I thought of how often it seemed we are tossed back and forth like the wind.

I deliberately switched my thoughts from what was being preached. I was concentrating deeply on how God loved me that He allowed His only son to die on the cross for me. I noticed everyone standing. I grabbed up the hymnal, jumped to my feet, peeked over the shoulder of the person in the balcony row in front of me for the page number, flipped to the page, and started singing. Once again, I was in deep meditation on the words of the song. Suddenly, I felt a quivering wave going over the inside and outside of my body. Tears rolling down my cheeks, I sang the words as a prayer, "Father, God, I surrender all to You. I committed my whole being to God. No matter what, I did not care about any denominational belief — I just knew that I loved God with all of my being, and I was willing to surrender all of myself to Him. That was the beginning of my personal search for the word of God to manifest itself in my heart. I decided I will find God for myself and not rely on the speculations and uncertainties of man.

One day in my search for spiritual fulfillment, I went to a revival of a "holiness" persuasion. It was my research project. I wanted to know about healing and getting "slain" in the spirit. At the outdoor meeting, emotions were high, and people were vocal with "Amens," "Praise God's," "Hallelujah's," etc. When a prayer line was formed, I had my doubts. Oh, I had doubts the whole time I was there, but I got in the prayer line anyway to gather solid facts for my research — you know, just in case. I watched closely at the presiding Holy Ghost-filled evangelistic touching, praying, and pushing. Yes, I see why people were falling out. I didn't want to judge. After all, I was young, and all this charismatic stuff was new to me, but "fake" was a recurring word in my mind.

Before it was my turn to face the big, heavy hand that looked as though my entire head could fit in its palm, I made up my mind to stand my ground and not be forced down. I mean, really: I may not know much, but I do know God is real and doesn't play games! My turn came. When I didn't fall from the pressure on my forehead, I felt one hand on my shoulder and another hand heavy on my head, moving my head back and forth, shaking me like a rag doll. I stood my ground, repositioning my feet a couple of times to keep my balance. I saw the sisters on each side of me with outstretched sheets, just waiting for me to fall. Not today! I thought everyone else can "shake and fake," but God is not going to be disappointed in me.

My arms were stretched out and my hands turned up. I was praying to God to genuinely fill me with His Holy Spirit if it's real and, at the same time, I was determined that this person was not going to make me fall to the ground. Suddenly, I realized that there was no sound — just complete quiet — and, then, what

Will I Praise You, Lord, for Blessings From Above?

seemed like a haze of light engulfed me. I started floating backwards in slow motion. I don't know how long I lay there. When I felt my eyelids fluttering, I realized I was on the ground, and people were around me, rubbing my hands and fanning me. I felt so embarrassed, but it took another few minutes — that seemed like an eternity — to move. I was so upset with myself for being carried away with emotionalism. As I tried to regain my composure, hands were lifting me to my feet. It was absolutely time to go.

The group I came with chattered all the way back to the drop-off point. I didn't say a word, not wanting to be numbered among the fakers — but I felt like one. I don't speak of the incident; it happened when I was young and impressionable. However, at times, it comes back to mind as a questionable occurrence. Was it real? Is there such a thing as being "slain in the spirit"? This experience opened up a bushel basket running over with questions. I have not read in the Bible anywhere about being "slain" in the spirit — people "falling out" in this manner. However, I have read of being baptized in the Spirit and wondered if it was the same.

Can one be baptized in the Spirit and it (Holy Spirit) lie dormant in their life for years? Or perhaps the Holy Spirit is waiting for that individual to acknowledge God fully in their life. I asked another question: Is this the same as changing from glory to glory, being transformed into the image of Jesus Christ? If so, is being filled with the Spirit having God with you *at all times* — not once a week, but every day? Then, if so, should not every day with God be a transforming process? And, if so, it seems we are in the presence of God. Walking in the Spirit and not fulfilling sins of the flesh leads to sanctification. The thing about sanctification and righteousness is that I can't see them being put on and taken off like a Sunday dress-up-in-your-best-suit. You wear certain ties only with certain suits and certain jewelry with certain dresses. Is God an ornament that you put on with your Sunday dress-up-in-your-best-attire, and, then, when you come home, you take it off, not to be worn again until it appeals to your taste at the next Sunday dress-up? Wow! This may take a lifetime of searching. I probed for answers to these internal questions as I sought to grow closer to God. I looked back over my life to see how God kept me in His way — known and unknown.

Here's another example of research to find God for myself.

I often laugh at the time, years later, when I went alone to the downtown church. A group of co-workers, about four or five of us, wanting to have Bible study or prayer on our lunch break, would walk the two blocks to the church building. The double doors stood spread open all day, inviting the public to enter. This time, I was alone. I entered and walked straight to the altar, where I knelt. No one was there.

This time, I was seeking to speak in tongues. I prayed and cried, believing what I was told — that I was not spirit-filled unless I spoke in tongues. I was told just to start speaking gibberish and that it would turn into tongues. I didn't understand, since I thought speaking in tongues *was* speaking gibberish. It was explained to me that, although it may *sound* like gibberish to me, it is a spiritual language that only God understands, a heavenly language. I wasn't going to speak in gibberish — I thought that would be trying to fool God.

So, I simply lifted my hands toward the heavens, saying, "Hallelujah!" For about 45 minutes, I sang and prayed the power of God down. Suddenly, without a thought to what I was going to say, two unknown words jumped from my mouth. My mind did not process these words or translate them through the normal speech sensory mechanism of my brain. The two words jumped out of my mouth without thought. Possible? I left the church elated that God loved me so much that He listened to my foolish heart and blessed me with two words in tongue. Content that God had shown Himself to me, I have not sought to speak in tongues again. Soon, those spiritual words, which I had once considered a matter of life and death, disappeared from my memory just as they had appeared. Do I believe in tongues? I believe in God and that He does whatever He chooses to do, whenever and however He sees fit to make Himself known.

Oh, there are plenty of other times when God let me know He was carrying me through life's ups and downs. Once, faced with foreclosure, I sought housing for myself and my three children. This is when we were living in a three-bedroom house with a big front yard and a double-the-size, fenced-in back yard. I worked hard to make our house a loving home in spite of the absence of a husband and father. When I opened the mail from the mortgage company, I was shocked to read a foreclosure notice. I called to learn that my estranged husband had not made the house payment for five months.

Well, there was no way I would be put out of our home onto the streets. Once before, I had left my husband because I thought I could not handle it anymore. Guess what? I quickly came to my senses after three days of living with my parents. I started quoting scriptures centered mainly around the theme that God had not given me the spirit of fear but of power, love, and a sound mind. "I said, "So here I am again, Lord. Help me, please. I started searching the papers and apartment buildings for places to live. I remember the last straw.

I drove miles northward from our home to an apartment building that was in my price range. The nice manager showed me around. The apartment felt closed-in — with only a small living room that would barely seat four; I could forget about entertaining any playmates of my three growing children. There was no space for a kitchen table for family dinner or to sit to do homework. The apartment was just too small and without character. I asked about the back yard. We went out the kitchen door and down some steps. There was no back yard; it was all concrete, no grass, no fence for protection against intruders. I left so disappointed.

As I drove the miles back to my home, with tears

rolling down my cheeks, anger started bubbling up in me. Why was I so willing to lie down without a fight? Am I not a Believer? Do I not have power in Jesus Christ? I gripped the steering wheel tighter. Are the scriptures not meant for me? Why should I uproot my children and disrupt their lives? Right then and there, I took a stand! I was not willing to take my girls from the only home they knew to a place that I considered an unsafe environment — where they could not even play outside without supervision. Now physically taking my anger out on the steering wheel, I hit it as I loudly asked, "Why on earth should I do that?"

I spoke boldly to God and reminded Him of His promises. I spoke those promises aloud; they flowed out of my mouth, one after the other. I told God I expected Him to keep every one of His promises to me because I was His child, committed to him. By the time I got home, I had worked myself up to show God that, from this minute on, I would be a bold solider for Him to lead in the fight. I continued the one-sided dialogue, stripping off my clothes as I spoke. Naked, I threw myself before Him on the green-carpeted floor in my front room, humbling myself and asking Him to direct me to what I needed to do to stay in my house.

When I became utterly exhausted, with no more words or tears left, I got up, dusted myself off, and got busy. Forget calling the mortgage company again — I knew HUD (U. S. Department of Housing and Urban Development) owned our house. I got their number from the Yellow Pages and called. After being transferred several times, I finally got the correct department. As I explained how and why I was in this situation, I realized I needed to put things in writing. I asked for the address to mail my letter. I wrote a detailed but brief and to-the-point letter asking for a hearing. I heard back from them within two weeks. I went to the hearing and was granted mortgage arrangements. That was 38 years ago. Two refinances later, I am still in my home!

God honored me with His presence. He showed up! He is always there for me and for anyone who gives their life to Him.

Life

It was such a beautiful, unseasonably warm Friday evening. The girls were with my cousin Mary for the weekend. I had no plans. I was just happy to be free — not from my wonderful kids, but free emotionally and mentally. Not knowing what to do with this freedom, I decided to wash my car. I went to a car wash, and there were 20 to 30 other vehicles in line, waiting for their turns at one of the four stalls. The wait should not be more than 30 minutes, I figured. I finally pulled up to the car vacuum. I was excited. I was actually doing something I had not done in years. I felt so much better than I had in months. I had a new lease on life that kept me moving and feeling better about myself.

I cleaned my car out with vigor, swiftly and thoroughly. I think my vigor impressed the man in the aisle next to mine. He started talking to me about the weather, the many people out to wash cars, my car, and his car. I was reserved but cordial — you never know who will end up receiving the gospel of Christ. He finished vacuuming; since the people ahead of us both were still washing their car, he came over to finish his conversation. He introduced himself as Will. After a few minutes, the car behind Will honked for his attention.

The person in front of Will was pulling out of the stall. Will said he would help me dry my car off and to go ahead and get the extra wax. I had not been to a car wash for a long time. My black, sleek, curvy Neon that I had named "Neonna" was a bit dirty and deserved all my pampering because of my neglect. True to his word, Will was waiting when I pulled out. Ignoring my protest, he pulled out a shammy and got busy. We hit it off right away. It felt good laughing, talking about our favorite songs, movies, and restaurants. Though Will did most of the talking, I flashed a bragging smile at him when he said he bowled. I had not been bowling in years, but the last time I had gone, my average was 135 — not too bad.

The conversation continued. I was surprised when he

asked — before I did — what I call "the defining question."

"What church do you attend?" was a significant question, but much more meaningful was the invitation extended to attend service that Sunday. I was very impressed. This led me to turn the conversation toward spiritual matters. I asked him what his beliefs were. This question generally stuns one into silence for a few seconds followed by bewilderment about what the answer should be. Not so with Will. I let him go on for two minutes before I interrupted. I had heard enough to know that I would be comfortable in worship service at his church. However, I thanked him and informed him that I needed to be at my church for a special meeting that Sunday but that I would be glad to come another time.

Suddenly, he started humming as he polished the side mirrors. When he finished, we both studied Neonna with seriousness, deciding she was in "Cadillac" condition. I thanked him for all his excellent detailing skills. Then I said, "I think I will spit-shine Neonna every Friday." We shook hands and departed ways. I felt good about having such a light, friendly, and informal conversation with a man. Because he did not ask for my name or number, I decided he was just being friendly, with no ulterior motives. I was relieved. I was not interested in being "hit on" and feeling that awkwardness when you have to explain why you are not interested. I had no additional time to spend outside my family. There were years I needed to make amends for to my girls.

With God's help, I started gradually changing my way of living on the couch every day — simply by not being there as much. I decided that, in order for weekends to be all about my kids, I would do laundry in the mornings during the week, and, each evening, I cleaned and did things I used to do (or should have been doing) on the weekends. Memorable Family Experience (MFE) started Friday evening. Rain changed my plans from taking the girls to the carwash the next Friday, so I made Bible study fun. I promised myself to make every weekend an

Will I Praise You, Lord, for Blessings From Above?

MFE. I informed my three girls that this weekend's agenda was Saturday-morning breakfast at the Pancake House, Saturday-afternoon carwash, then home again with card and board games, Sunday School lesson review and then preparations for church. I told them we would be visiting another church after Sunday school at our church.

They had many questions. I could tell they were excited. I was glad about this. I like to show my girls how to embrace new experiences as adventures to knowledge. We looked forward to visiting a new church as long as the preacher didn't single us out to prove his calling as a prophet or some kind of medium for tongues. I really liked the church we were attending regularly then, but, at times, I liked venturing out.

We arrived at Freedom in Christ Church. When we stepped through the door, we were greeted with smiles, hugs, "God bless you," and "Thank you for coming." One sister even said, "Make yourselves at home." I loved that, because, to me, it spoke of family and the comfort you feel being among family. There was a mutual feeling of trust that neither they nor us would feel uncomfortable (it was a love-sharing experience). My girls were smiling as they walked and shook hands. It didn't matter that they were kids; people were shaking their hands as if they were just as happy to see them as they were me. We felt welcome as we came through the door, not overpowering or insincerely, but genuinely welcomed.

I followed the girls to our seats. They knew I like to sit closer to the front on the inside aisle. After five minutes, the praise team gathered, and we were off. The singing was melodious, and the choice of songs was meaningful in encouraging, edifying, and elevating spiritual worship to God. The instruments were not at the center of the music but actually were played as accompaniments. I enjoyed being able to hear the words of the song. These musicians know the words are what bring on the praise to God and not the banging of noise. No one made you feel uncomfortable if you were not standing, dancing, or running. Yes, I have been to a few churches when the minister said, "Run for the Lord," and people would take off running around the room. Please don't misunderstand. If the Holy Spirit moves you in your heart to run, then you should run. Just make sure your worship to God is in Spirit and truth.

As I looked around the sanctuary, some people were standing, most were rocking from side to side in their seat, some heads were bowed, eyes closed, hands waving, clapping. Everyone was praising God but everyone in their own way — even if they were only sitting in their seats singing. I could hear the love, sincerity, and depth of emotion that lifted up to the heavens. There was a freedom and comfort of open praise.

I absolutely loved the flow from the praise team in preparation of the heart for the Word of God. There was no interruption when the minister picked up singing the last song and went directly into the message from God. The Word was preached with boldness — points were made from the main scripture and then broken down and backed up with reference scriptures. The message was easy to follow and to understand — not flowered-up with frilly words or obscure words that required a dictionary to understand. I knew my girls understood, so I made a mental note to ask them about points made in the message. Directly after the message came the communion. Again, the flow was uninterrupted, and the significance placed on the Lord's Supper brought it all home to why worship should be every day.

Then the visitors were asked to stand for recognition. The members who had greeted us at the door popped up from where they were sitting and rushed over to introduce us. A different young girl introduced each of my girls without reading from visitor cards — and the same with me. The first girl said, "Church family, this is Charlotte, who is 14 and likes to cook." The second girl said, "Church family, this is Carla, who is 11 and tries to stay out of trouble, but her smile gives her away." Then the third girl said, "Everybody, this is Caira, who is 9 and likes to have her friends sleep over at her house."

Then the sister who introduced me stated that Brother Willyndro Prestin had invited us. My mouth dropped because I had forgotten all about Will. Everyone turned around, looking upward, toward the back of the auditorium; I looked as well to see him wave from a booth in the balcony. Obviously, it was the recording booth, since he had on a headset. He spoke through the microphone: "Sister Janice and daughters, Mr. and Mrs. Marcus, Elbert Finney, and Sister Barbara and anyone else visiting us today, thank you for making the choice to visit with us here at Freedom in Christ. We are blessed by your presence. We hope your spiritual experience this morning was truly a liberating one that will enhance your love for God. Please plan to come back soon." After the clapping and the chorus of "Amens!" ended, he said, "Charlotte, Carla, and Caira — please don't leave without letting me personally thank you for coming." Everyone clapped again. Clearly, he was serving in a dual capacity. I smiled when my girls gave him a wave. Then they looked at me, and, with obvious meaning, raised their eyebrows and smiled.

Just as we finished visiting with seemingly everyone, Will came over, standing next to me and talking with my girls. I sized him up quickly: About 35, five-feet-nine-and-a half-inches tall, 185 pounds, clear complexion, skin color two shades from dark chocolate, a slight beer belly, sideburns too thick and untrimmed, just like his unkempt hair and beard. Nope, friendly enough, but his appearance, though clean, neat, and semi-stylish, spoke, "Issues," "Baggage," and "Run!" Yet, his blue pin-stripe suit with matching tie, shining shoes, and manicured fingernails said there was a small margin for hope. Typical of Carla's character, she whispered loudly to Charlotte and Caira, "Uh, what's up with him?"

Just then, before she could say more, a five-foot-six tall female with a milk-caramel complexion, shoulder-length hair with brownish-blond streaks, stepped intrusively into the small circle, wrapping her arm around Will's arm. The female spoke rudely. The three of us said "Bye" at the same time, except Carla, who said, with attitude, "See ya." We turned quickly and left. We waited until we got in the car and then burst out in uncontrollable laughter. That woman had made it obvious she was claiming her property as if we were trespassing. We talked about that all the way to cousin Mary's house, where we revisited the whole thing with her over dinner. I told the girls that, if I saw Mr. Will again, I hope they'd be with me so that he could hear firsthand from them all the adjectives they used in describing his facial expression. They were hilarious! We burst out again, this time, with Mary laughing to tears.

Well as Missouri weather goes, it was five weeks later before we rolled into the car wash again. The girls hurried out of the car and started pulling Neonna's mats out. This time, I was at the tail end of the line. Twenty minutes later, I looked up and saw Will. He saw us and came over. He was in his jeans and short jacket again, but he was clean-shaven, trimmed up, and had a low hair cut that showed off a nice grade of hair — quite impressive. I said, "You clean up nicely. What made you shave?" He smiled and said, "Maybe one day I will tell you, but not now. He waved at the girls. They waved and kept working. They were having fun spraying each other with water. Car washing was not something they did very often.

Will picked up from the last time we saw each other, speaking as if it had been just yesterday. He apologized with embarrassment for the scene on that Sunday. He started explaining that Jessica had problems and that he and the congregation were helping her. She had formed a misplaced attachment not only to him but to several other members, including females. What Will said next surprised me. It seems that our visit to his church had served a special purpose. It opened up dialogue with Jessica that would not have happened had we not been there. He said that, after we left, several of the church members met with her to explain what she did and told her that it was not proper. Everyone had been walking on eggshells, Will said, trying to avoid doing anything that would cause Jessica to go off the deep end. However, the incident on that Sunday called for firm action.

Will said, "Church members and other visitors saw and heard Jessica's aggressive stepping between us causing you to lose your balance to the point that your kids had to keep you from falling, and her gruff comment for you to leave because I was *her* man was the last straw. We just cannot allow people to be chased away because of our fear to confront a potential volatile situation!" Will stated that, absolutely, I was a Godsend and that he would like us to consider coming back to visit soon.

I pulled the car out of the stall to the wipe-down area, and Will helped. The girls started to clown with him about his name, Willyndro. Will laughed at the skewed pronunciations of his name. "Some people called me Will. Family call me Lyn, but I am seldom called Willyndro," he said. Carira asked, "Who calls you Dro?" He said, "Well, that would be special; if you like, you can call me "Dro." I quickly added, "*Mister* Dro." He turned to me and said, "I will call you "Ice," short for Jan*ice,* since you were so cold the first time we met. I was shocked, thinking I had been friendly. I said jokingly, "Consider yourself privileged you got *that* much conversation from me — you being a complete stranger."

We, in turn, helped wash Will's car. Then Will treated us all to lunch at the nearby McDonald's. It was at McDonald's that the girls spoke of the details of the incident at Will's church with "that lady." We laughed until we cried. Will pulled a white handkerchief from his pocket to wipe the tears away. *How hearty and genuine his laughter sounded,* I thought.

After the girls were in bed, I called Cousin Mary. "He asked me to go to the drive-in," I told Mary over the phone. "I think the drive-in is too intimate, so we agreed to meet at a restaurant first and then go to the AMC theatre. Mary agreed. I couldn't believe I would be going on a *date* — the first date in 15 years. "That's because you had issues," Mary stated, "but this is the right time for you to get out amongst adults again. She was as excited as I was, volunteering to keep the girls — even before I asked. The date could not come soon enough.

Finally, the time arrived. I could not believe I was so nervous. I walked into the restaurant two minutes late. Will was sitting at the bar. As I walked up to him, I stated, "Some Christians would not approve of you sitting at a bar sipping Sprite on the rocks — let your good intentions not be spoken evil of." He laughed and said, "Let their judgment of me be betwixt them and God." He asked me if I had problems with drinking wine. I said, "Yes, in excess, but I can handle one glass with dinner." He smiled approvingly as if saying, "That was a good answer." I thought to myself: That answer didn't come from me.

We laughed all evening, over dinner and the romantic comedy we watched at the movies. The evening turned out to be relaxing and fun, even with an undercurrent of reserve.

One day, two weeks later, I ran to the phone, catching it on the third ring. "Hello?" I said.

"Hello," said the somewhat-familiar voice. Is this Janice?"

"Yes it is."

"This is Jessica."

Well, I only vaguely knew only *one* Jessica. "Hello, Jessica. How can I help you?" all the while remembering the conversation Will and I had concerning her volatile state of emotions.

"I am calling to see if I can talk to Will."

It was 9:30 on Tuesday evening. "Jessica, Will is not here, and I don't know how to get in touch with him." I thought how strange it was that Will and I didn't have each other's phone number. "Are you all right?" I asked, trying to temper my voice.

Her voice suddenly became impatient. "Well, I just need to talk to him. I can't reach anyone else to talk to. Can I talk to you?"

"How can I help you, Jessica?"
"No, I need to talk to you in person."
"Jessica, how did you get my number?" There was about a three-second silence.
"I sometimes help with filing the visitors cards."

Remembering her aggression, my mind flashed back — no, there was no space asking for addresses. Just date, name, and phone numbers. *Good— she does not know where we live,* I thought. Her voice sounded more strained than before. "Jessica, I will try to contact the Pastor for you. I think his number is on the contact card the church gave us. Can you wait while I get it?"
"I know his number! He is not answering!" she snapped. "I need to talk with Will, or Mitchell, or somebody — now! I don't know what to do! They're coming, and I'm all alone. I don't know what to do! They always help me..." Then there was silence, followed by a screech. "No one cares — why should anyone help me?"

"Where are you, Jessica?"
"I'm at home."
"Where is that?" "You know — at Will's place."

I tried to keep my voice low and contained, showing only concern for her. "Jessica, can you give me the address? If you want me to come over to talk, I will need the address."

Click! The phone went dead.
I pushed redial on the phone, but there was no answer. I hurriedly searched for the contact card. I called the number. After several rings, someone answered.

"Hello," a voice said.
"Hello, is this Pastor Simpson?"
"Yes." The heavy male voice sounded breathless.
"My name is Janice. I visited your church about two and a

half months ago. Jessica just called me looking for Will. I think she might be in trouble."

There was about three seconds of silence, and then the voice said, "Yes, I remember you, Janice. Jessica is in trouble. Please pray for her. She is reaching out, but it's hard for her to let us help. Will is out of town on important personal manners. I don't see the necessity of further burdening him."

"What about Will or Mitchell?" I asked. "Jessica mentioned them, too."

"Myra, who was a case worker at our church, was able to get some information from her before she shut her out. Mitchell, is another case worker, is on his way and should be here soon. I just arrived home. I will leave in about 10 minutes to go to Jessica."

I took a deep breath. "Pastor, she did say she wanted to talk with me. Perhaps, in her mind, she's associating me with Will, and she thinks I can help.... I mean, there *is* a reason she called me."

There was about a six-second pause, and then the Pastor said, "If you speak with her, you will not be able to speak with her alone. I'm told she will not allow anyone in the house with her, so you may be talking through the door. Whatever the situation, we can talk to her caseworker, who is already there, when we get there. Okay, my dear, please pray about this on your way to my house. We will go together."

I wrote his address down.
He continued, "There are already members there, trying to talk with her through the door."
I hesitated before I asked, "Is she suicidal?"
"Yes."

A thought ran across my mind as I was driving to Pastor Simpson's house — "Let your mess become your message."

When we got to Jessica's home, she would not let anyone in but Mitchell and me. It was dim inside, with only one light on in the kitchen. We could see from across the room that Jessica was pacing side to side and that she had a knife in her hand. I was scared — not of the knife, but of saying or doing the wrong thing. Why on God's green earth did I volunteer for this? This is for me to watch on television — not be involved with in real life. I had never taken any counseling courses, but, thank God, Mitchell had. It turned out we were a good team, since we had both experienced depression. We instinctively followed each other's lead. It was not easy, with Jessica screeching, crying, and threatening.

My mind went back to younger adult years and my best friend, Milly, who I eventually had to take to the psychiatric unit. It was hard to see my best friend in such turmoil. I understood some of it, but, because I didn't live in her household, I am sure I didn't know the half of what Milly had to deal with as a child. I hurt even now thinking about the difficult things she had to deal with. One of the things I loved about my best friend was her compassion for others. My compassion for Jessica suddenly became overwhelming.

Mitchell did most of the talking, while I did the empathizing; since I myself had been suicidal at one time, I could speak to that issue. Jessica was raving and not making sense. I carefully asked her about family and children. She started to space out and started behaving in a slightly different way. "Okay," I thought to myself, "now we know what we are dealing with — family issues. "Stay calm," I told myself. Then, suddenly, Jessica calmed down and started sobbing softly as she related her life to us and that her only child hated her. There was a soft knock at the door. I quietly opened the door ever so slightly, while Mitchell diverted Jessica's attention. It was Myra, who informed me that they were able to contact Jessica's daughter, Brianna, who had told Myra she would be there in the morning from Virginia. I told Myra to have Brianna call my number in 10 minutes.

I eased back to Mitchell's side. I whispered to him about Brianna's call. Then I took the opportunity to reveal to Jessica that I, too, had once felt worthless, unloved, and so very much alone in a room full of people. I shared with Jessica that, one day, while I was walking downtown, I was so distraught as I walked through the busy streets that I could not see myself going through another miserable day. I explained to Jessica that the only thing that had kept me living up to that point was the joy of my girls. God knew exactly how to get through to me. He flashed a picture of my kids across my mind's eye, and then He asked me this question: "If you die, who will take care of *your* girls?" With that question, I hesitated, and that hesitation saved my life. It gave the people behind me a second to pull me out from in front of the fast-approaching traffic, giving the metro bus driver the same split second to swerve from hitting me as I deliberately stepped off the curb. Without a moment's thought, I said to Jessica, "God is asking you that same question, Jessica." I don't know why I said that and almost bit my lip. Jessica looked at me with either bewilderment or disbelief in her eyes — I could not figure out which.

While I had her attention, I hurried on, saying, "We spoke with your daughter, Brianna. Jessica, your daughter loves you so much that she is coming here to see you. She wants to see you. She will be here in the morning. Brianna will call you in a few minutes on my cell phone to talk with you. Jessica stared at us in disbelief. "You lie!" she shouted. "I haven't spoken to her in 15 years. She hates me; she hates me, and that's why she hasn't called — that's why she never calls!" And then, just as she was raising the knife to her chest, the phone rang, and she froze. Mitchell calmly whispered to me; "Let me handle it from here." I was so relieved that I felt my knees buckle. "Not yet — it's not over," I told myself, regaining strength. Mitchell answered the phone quickly, saying, "Brianna, Jessica needs to know who you are." He explained to Brianna that he was going to put her on speakerphone.

Brianna said, through sobs, "Mom, it's Brianna May, but, remember, I didn't like 'Brianna May,' so we made a pact that, whenever you called me by my full name, you would call me 'Briannalyn.' You told me we needed to spell it like it is one name, not two, so you spelled it B-r-i-a-n-n-a-l-y-n. Mom, remember when you were trying to teach me how to make gravy? You showed me three times, and, on the fourth try, you left me alone by myself to make it, and, when you came back, I had fixed a skillet full of what you called 'mud.' I had used almost all the flour. First, you were mad, and then you tasted it and said, "We will freeze it. Just a tablespoon full of this mud will make enough good gravy to feed a whole family. We laughed so hard, we fell to the floor. Mom," the shaky voice said with tenderness, "you have two beautiful granddaughters who can't wait to love on you. I miss you so much, Mom. I will be down in the morning to get you."

Jessica gave a loud cry of released anguish, dropped the knife, and fell to her knees, covering her face with her hands, as tears squeezed through her fingers and ran down, streaking her arms. I kicked the knife across the room, dropped to my knees, wrapped my arms around her shoulders, and cried with her. "See, Jessica? God wants you here to help take care of your beautiful granddaughters." Mitchell finished the call to Briannalyn off speaker.

That Sunday, the girls and I went to Pastor Simpson's church. When Pastor Simpson called to invite me to Freedom In Christ, I told him I do feel a need to come but to please not mention me separately — we all were where God would have us be, acting as a team. As we walked into the sunny, colorful vestibule, members greeted us. It was a more personal greeting than before. Everyone one was hugging one another. There were so many tears, tight hugs, and handshakes that the service started 15 minutes late. Will came up and hugged me, with tears in his eyes. I said, "Let's talk later." He nodded. I had not seen or spoken to Will since our date two weeks earlier. I dismissed the thought from my mind, not allowing myself to ask why.

My spirit truly connected with the Spirit of God throughout the service. The Pastor spoke wonderfully of Jessica and the members who had helped her over the past year she had been with them. He explained openly about her perverted childhood and how it was God's plan for families to break the generational curses. Having her only child, a 10-year-old, taken from her by the child's father, along with the demons that her mother had embedded in her during childhood, had sent her on an emotional roller-coaster ride.

After worship, my girls asked if they could go with the other kids to the vending machines in the fellowship hall. Will and I followed and sat down at the table opposite the vending machines, where we could talk and watch the kids. After a minute of straining to hear each other, Will pulled out two dollars to give them so they would not have to argue over how they would spend the one dollar they had. They settled down contentedly, talking as they ate their treats.

I related the events of Tuesday, starting with the call from Jessica.

When I completed explaining the events to Will, he said he was sorry he had not been there for Jessica but was glad I was there in his place. He explained that Jessica felt some sort of connection with him, since his name reminded her of her daughter, and she sometimes called him Lyn, short for Willyndro. I informed Will that Jessica's caseworker had said that her mental and emotional state connected me with him. That's why she was okay with speaking to me and that she was subconsciously sorry for her outburst and show of territorial aggression toward me at church. Will surmised that, since Jessica thought we were a couple, she thought we must be of the same mind and that, therefore, she could talk with me as if I could relate to her as he could. That puzzled me, since I did not know why she thought we were a couple. I asked why would she say she was at his place. Will said that he owned the four-plex, and, when one of the

Will I Praise You, Lord, for Blessings From Above?

apartments became available, he let her move in last year because she did not have a place to stay. Before we left, he asked, "Can I have your phone number?"

That night, over the phone, I told Mary that Will had finally asked for my phone number and that I had given it to him. She was so excited that she just about had us courting. I told her I didn't think so. There was something off. I had that same sense of reserve that I had before. Something was not quite right. I could not put my finger on it, but it was definitely there. When Will called an hour later, he told me the reason he had been out of town. His ex-wife of two years had cancer, and there was no one to help her. He said that he would be moving down to Abilene, Texas, in the next week. He still loved her and needed to be there for her. I asked him if I could pray for his wife, Sarah, and him. We prayed.

Power 'n' 24/7 Praise

A Unique Privilege Granted to Me

My cousin, who is my mother's niece and best friend, called me "Neet" as a nickname. She was the only one who called me "Neet," which is a shorter variation of my middle name. Of course, this made me feel special. I loved Cousin Rose all my life. She was a gentle, soft-spoken person, but she could get loud and firm but keep a soft tone — all at the same time. This made her seem more like my auntie than my cousin. I guess she had to be firm, since she, as well as my Mom, had to manage their households, raise their children, and satisfy their husbands.

Because of the closeness between Cousin Rose and my Mom, I was often over to her house for one reason or another. When I was younger, I could not understand how she was my cousin and not my aunt. I knew her mother was my aunt, but I guess the part I did not understand was that her mother, my mom's sister, and my mother's mother (Cousin Rose's grandmother) were pregnant at the same time. Mom and Cousin Rose delivered her son and me just several days apart. Cousin Rose would tell me how her son Ben, while playing in the same crib with me, would swipe my bottle. I would cry a little and snatch my bottle back, hit him with it, and watch him cry. I loved to hear stories about our childhood. Cousin was so much a part of our lives. At first, I didn't know she was sick. Mom said she thought she had told me. I think Momma was so upset about it that she didn't want to talk about it. I didn't know until several months into her sickness. As her sickness progressed, I started seeing little indications.

So, I just didn't know she was as sick as she was. I felt so guilty that I was not more attentive and more of a presence in the last year of her life. The only thing I could do for my Auntie-cousin was pray.

COMMERCIAL BREAK: "Prayer is an essential tool when you have nothing else. If you don't have prayer, I strongly suggest that you acquire it. How do you acquire prayer? There must be Faith — in God the Father, first and foremost, and in God the Son as your focus– and in God the Holy Spirit. Faith is the key element of prayer, in that, without it, there is no conversation with God".

END OF COMMERCIAL BREAK. We will resume with the story.

One day Mom called and told me Cousin was in the hospital. She had been there several days before I even knew. I visited her every day. I would go on my lunch break to read to her. Then they moved her to another room. This is when her children started coming into town. The family poured in. We had crying sessions and prayer sessions; we had walks down memory lane; we had encouragement and uplifting periods that gave brief relief. I was too afraid to leave. I wasn't going to leave. Then there was like a changing of the guard. Some of Cousin's other children were coming, and, so, the ones who had been there needed to go home for showers and changes of clothes. I told them I would stay.

I will never forget the time I procrastinated visiting Assistant Pastor Cox, who was in his 80s, while he was in the hospital. I was in my teens, and, since I had been driving only a few months, I made it my business to go everywhere. When I finally made time to go see Assistant Pastor Cox, the nurse at the desk had me repeat whom I was there to see, as if she had not heard me. Her expression changed as she spoke, using a word that I had not heard used in the sense she was using it — "…expired…." After seeing the bewilderment on my face, the nurse explained to me that he had died. My heart wrenched. Oh, I still feel the guilt of my conscience.

It took hard work to befriend old grumpy Assistant Pastor

Cox. I thought he needed a friend, so I made myself cheerful, ignoring his abruptness. It wasn't long before I had befriended him. Either I got used to his rudeness, or I won him over, but we had become close the last couple of years before his illness. Now, looking back, I realize he could have been ill all along, and that might have been what was making him so mean. Now, I have to live with the knowledge of not saying good-bye to my friend when I had the opportunity. He had few family members — most had already died. I felt I should have been there. I remember thinking, "There is very little that God asks me to do, and that I don't do." Two days prior to Assistant Pastor Cox's death, God placed it on my heart to visit him, and I didn't do it.

God placed it on my heart not to leave Cousin Rose. Everyone else had left. It seemed like only minutes alone with Cousin when her breathing changed. I called the nurse, who would not say anything but started coming in more frequently. I learned how to attend to the suction of mucus from Cousin's throat to keep her air passage clear. I was grateful I could do something to help her be comfortable. I continued this procedure whenever Cousin needed it. I was already talking to Cousin, but now I started singing some of the gospel songs I knew she liked. I no longer tried to be quiet and reserved when singing. I wanted to make sure she heard me sing, talk, and read the Bible to her. The nurses were in and out. On one of their visits, they asked me to step out. I thought they just didn't want to tell me to be quiet. Finally, after allowing me back in, they confirmed that she was in what some may call a "declining state," but I called it an "ascending state."

I had entered phone numbers in my cell phone before Cousin's children left. I started calling. "Hurry back" was the message I left if no one answered. "Hurry back" was the message if someone *did* answer. I had never seen death. At first, fear started to creep into my mind, but, through tears and with a shaky voice, I kept smiling, singing, and praying. I did not stop even when the nurses were coming in and out.

 **COMMERCIAL BREAK:** Have you had a prayer today? Having a conversation with God is a unique privilege that is taken for granted too often, perhaps because we, as Christians, are told to pray without ceasing, (I Thessalonians 5:17). However, when you think that the Creator of the universe and everything within it loves us so much that He provides an immediate-access system so that we can talk to him in an instant — Wow! Prayer becomes quite a bit more essential. If you are one of the many who ask others to pray for you because you don't feel adequate in getting a prayer through, remember, God wants to hear personally from **you!** God the Son is your only mediator to God the Father, and He is waiting for you to talk with Him on your own behalf. GET A PRAYER LIFE STARTED TODAY!"

COMMERCIAL BREAK OVER.

I prayed a prayer of thanksgiving to God for the privilege of being her cousin-niece. I prayed a prayer thanking God for loving her and keeping her through her life, especially through the rough times in her life that I knew about. Then, something amazing happened. Cousin opened her eyes and looked into mine. I was expecting her to say, "Hey, Neet" or sing with me, as we sometimes sang duets riding to and fro in the car. But Cousin didn't say anything. I smiled at her with all the love within me. As I pushed the button for the nurse, I wondered, did she know it was me? Could she even see? I am believing that she did and that she could, but, by the time the nurse came, Cousins' eyes were closed again. I told them what had happened. The nurse checked her vitals and said she may make it another hour. My auntie-cousin ascended 15 minutes later.

I thought to myself, as tears rolled down my cheeks, "It isn't important that she knew who I was — not at all." I prayed that she heard the songs and prayers on her way to heaven. Cousin was a person who was caring, sharing, and who believed in God the Father, God the Son, and God the Holy Spirit. I knew this because of our many personal conversations. She was faithful in attending worship service. Even when she *did* have a ride, at times she would call me and ask, "Neet — you going to church?" I would pick her up. I never knew her not to be kind. I believed she was this way because Cousin Rose loved God. I can see her singing in the choir, "I am on the battlefield for my Lord/and I promised Him that I would serve until I died/Yes I'm on the battlefield for my Lord." I can see Cousin standing tall, thrusting her left fist out, emphasizing with zeal her stand for Jesus. She would tell me, "Baby, God will see you through, yes, He will." God was faithful to Cousin. He saw her through to her new beginning.

To hold my auntie-cousin's hand while she took her last breath was a unique privilege and blessing of a special kind that I will never forget.

Old Soldiers, New Soldiers

Old Soldiers, new soldiers, all Christian soldiers
Are faithful, Intense, ready to stand firm
On the battlefield of spitting bullets of immorality,
Blowing fire of dishonesty, hailing grenades of apathy.
We stand strong in the fight when the raging rages harder
We fight harder. We fight on in faith. We press on to win.
The victory is at hand.
We follow the Mighty Leader;
we do not simply flail the air with our fists.
Our blows land firmly for righteousness.
We know the weapons of our warfare are mighty with
Promise to defeat our enemy.
We fight with the light that dispels darkness.
We fight, always abounding in the work of The Lord
We fight in readiness to avenge all disobedience
When obedience is fulfilled
We fight, bringing into captivity every thought to the
Obedience of Christ.
We fight with Love. God Is Love.
The victory is at hand.
Old soldiers, new Soldiers, all Christian soldiers
Are faithful, intensely planted in an
imperishable stand.

Death

How do you handle death? How do you live through death of a loved one? Or is the question really, "What is death to you?"

You handle death as you do any other significant life-altering occurrence in your life. Acknowledge it for what it is, take care of it in the manner necessary, and it is over with until the next event or occurrence, unless you die as well.

How do you live through the death of a loved one? You take it to God. Pour out your feelings to God — all of them. Tell how you loved this person and why, how sometimes you disliked or hated this person and why. God knows all "loved" ones are not loved all the time. There are peaks and valleys in a love relationship — be it a son, daughter, mother, father, sister, or brother, etc. Tell God all — He knows it anyway. Because He knows, it makes talking to Him more consoling than talking to anyone else. You can even tell God why you are now talking to Him when perhaps you haven't for months or years — or ever. That is one reason God allows death — to bring the living closer to Him.

Talk to God every day about your loss. Tell Him why you feel like it is a loss. Tell God why you don't believe in Heaven or Hell. Tell God why you believe Heaven and Hell are here on Earth. Tell God how you know more than He does. Tell him why you think you will be an atheist from here on out. Once you get through talking to God and sharing everything in your heart, tell Him that you will listen as He now speaks back to you. If you don't want God to speak to you through the Bible, let Him speak to you through His creation. Hear Him tell you of his power, wisdom, and infinite love for you and your loved one — and that he created all this beauty for you. Listen as God tells you that the cold of winter helps you appreciate the heat of summer and that the beauty of fall helps you appreciate the growth of spring. Hear God tell you the death of your loved one helps you appreciate the life and death of His only begotten Son — His Son, whom he knowingly and willingly gave to die so that you could have eternal life with him, because He knows that, one day, you, too, will face death. Hear Him tell you that it is a subtle trick of The Adversary to get you in his clutches by telling you that God does not care, therefore, there is no God.

How do you see death? Some see death as a closed door never to open again — an eternal void and unconsciousness. There are all kinds of belief. If you are of the Christian faith, you know that the Son of God took the sting from death by His life of sinless living. His sinless life made it possible for him to die in our place, as our substitute. He sacrificed himself for us. Jesus the Christ was atonement for us because we were full of sin. We were as filthy rags, unable to stand before a righteous and just God. The price for sin is a spiritual separation from God. This means that, if you die in sin, you cannot be in the presence of the Holy God — you are bound to Hell.

This is a choice given to you — an option made available for your decision. God has made the gift of salvation free. Salvation is a release from the chains of sin in this life to a glorious life with him in the next life. The gift of salvation is yours only if you truly believe that Jesus is the Son of God. You must believe He lived on this Earth a sinless life, that He died on the cross of Calvary, that He was buried, that He rose from the dead, and that He ascended to God the Father to take his place at God's right hand, where He is mediating on your behalf to God. There is nothing other than believing this gospel of Jesus Christ that you must do to obtain salvation. Tell God what is in your heart. For example, say, "God, I believe in You and all that Your word says about Your son Jesus the Christ. I believe Jesus the Christ died for me, was buried, and rose again on the third day, as I read in the scriptures. I am sorry I have lived my life in sin. I repent of my sins, and I give my life completely to you. Thank You for loving me and helping me to live a life free from the desire to sin. In Jesus' name. Amen."

Now, this is me handling death.
What death?

My son was 22 when the drive-by shooter shot him dead. Ricky was out on the streets at midnight, walking back from the corner gas station to the apartment he was staying at. In that area of town, it was not a good idea to be out that late, but, like I said, he was 22. His life was in turmoil. He loved strongly, and he hated strongly. Keeping it real, I am sure he smoked weed at times. He was always busy due to ADHD, always wired up, so I can't say he was never on a high when he was around me. However, I would know "high" when I saw it. I was familiar with addiction by way of Ricky's father.

Ricky was loving and compassionate. It was very hard for me to let him go when death came. I knew God, in His infinite wisdom, always allowed things such as death to happen for a reason. Sometimes Ricky would grab me up in his long, lanky arms and hug me tight. With his mouth buried in my neck, he would muff out "I love you, Momma." I would laugh and cry at the same time since his breath and big, thick lips tickled my neck. At times, he would sit and listen to me talk to him about God. Sometimes, as soon as I started, he would plant a sloppy wet kiss on my cheek and take off running, looking back at me with a big grin on his face, showing all his white teeth.

If Ricky loved you and you were in need, he would give you what you need if it was within his power — usually out of my house. I often wondered, "Where did that pot go?" or "Where is that blanket?" One time, he walked home in the cold without his coat. I always wondered if he forgot to get it or if he had given it away. He was like that, thinking he could get another one, whereas they couldn't. However, if he didn't like you, he would have nothing to do with you unless you made him mad. Then, he would tell you to your face what he thought about you.

I remember one proud Sunday, a couple of people at the church made derogatory remarks to Ricky. It seemed to be the attitude of most of the members in the small family church to do that. Ricky waited until the invitation, and he went down front. When it was Ricky's turn, I held my breath, not knowing what my son would do or say. But when he looked at me, I smiled and nodded for him to say what he needed to say, because I knew he was not a disrespectful child. He got angry only when it was justified. It was his ability to control himself that was the uncertainty. He stood and told the entire church about their attitude and how he felt it was wrong. He said just what was in his heart and took his seat. I was thankful no one interrupted or tried to stop him, which would definitely have caused him to lose control. Some members were offended, some pensive, and some repentant. I was so proud of him that he handled his emotions and allowed his anger to channel out in a positive way. Ricky was loveable most of the time — but a hard person for most people to love and deal with when he was angry, and he *was* an angry teenager.

Why was Ricky an angry teenager? Childhood sexual abuse by a family member and an absentee druggie father were a couple of reasons for Ricky's anger. However, even with all of that, Ricky was *not* 24/7 angry. There were many good and happy times.

It may be hard for some to understand why Ricky's death was bittersweet for me and maybe for his siblings as well. Because Ricky would not take his medication for his ADHD, I believe life was very hard for him. Because of the ADHD, Ricky dropped out of school at 16. This was also bittersweet, since he was in constant trouble, and the public school system was clueless as to how to address the needs of such brilliant students. Life became difficult. Ricky tried so hard to find a job, and, when he did, he could not keep it. My heart broke for him so many times knowing how hard he tried to fit in. He cried to me on a few occasions, asking, "Why me?" I tried different things that I hoped would help. Ricky had doubts, but he went along with it, either because he wanted it to work so badly or because he just wanted to appease me — I don't know.

Will I Praise You, Lord, for Blessings From Above?

One time, Ricky walked into my house (he lived in and out) with street-length garb on. He saw how seriously upsetting this was to me. I knew he had friends and was hanging out around people who believed in that way of life. So now, I'm thinking they had converted him over. He said something that I will always treasure in my heart. "Momma, I remember everything you taught me, and I believe in what you taught me. I may wear this, but I know what is what — I know the real deal." Because of that, I know I will see Ricky again after my death, after my departure from this life. I thank Jesus for His life and death to make our eternal life in heaven possible.

It is easier to live without a loved one when you have Christ as your Savior. Even now, I hurt as I remember back to the good and bad times with my son. I almost stopped writing this twice, thinking, "I can't do this." But I want to encourage who I can by sharing my story with you.

It was devastating to see my baby boy, my youngest child, lying on the cold, concrete sidewalk. The police would not let me near him to hold him, to rock him, to say, "I love you, and God has you now." My son could not hear me say, "Goodbye, Ricky — I'll love you forever." I cried my heart out in the arms of the police officer who was holding me back. My other son, emotionally distraught because he had just found out his little brother was dead, jumped out of his car, and ran in bewildered disbelief. He was not allowed time to get his emotions in check. The police pounced on him, wrestled him to the ground, threatening to take him downtown to jail. My mind jumped from Ricky's still, lifeless body lying on the ground to Rusty's squirming body on the ground, trying to get the five police officers' knees and feet off of his back, thighs, and ankles. In other words, I had to leave the dead to attend to the living — and that is what life is about.

I thank God Ricky is liberated from this world and is presently with God in heaven. Even if your loved one was perfect in your sight, not at all like Ricky, their life and death — just as ours — are all in God's hands, so the best we can do with death is to encourage the living to live life the way it was intended by God, so that, when death happens, it is just a step into a better place. *Learn now what true worship of God is.*

Reality

What is the real reality of dreams?
The reality of dreams is that dreams stay within
The realm of dreams is a myth
Sure you can dream — daydreams or night dreams
But when you wake, you deal with reality
This is the reality of dreams
and the realness of reality
If reality is the dream you can make come true,
What is the reality of dreaming, or are dreams
Placed here by God for us to make into reality?
I had a daydream that somehow melted into reality.
It was a daydream or vision — I don't know which
Of a young life lost,
Déjà vu? No, the daydream became reality
I saw my son lying on the cold concrete
In both dream and reality.
My son's life was a reality, and, now, that's a dream
God was making dreams reality.
Or, was I dreaming reality?
Why would God allow me to see this before it happened?
His MERCY is REAL

Ricky

I hung his pictures on the wall
and threw him a big kiss
each time I passed.
His grin was so broad and contagious
I could not help but smile back.
Tears filled my eyes.
Will this river ever run dry?
Is there always sunshine after the rain?
I opened one of many envelopes
given to me when he was killed
And took out a five-dollar bill.
I saw his grin, his eyes looking at me,
I felt him say,
"I told you I'd pay you back some day."
I laughed and cried and then replied,
"Yeah, you
Nickeled and dimed me so tough, it's about time
You returned a buck."
Is there always sunshine after the rain?
Does joy come in the morning to diminish the pain?
Three pictures on the wall,
A carefree child with a mischievous smile.
I lashed out at those who would say, "bay-bay"
"No, don't give my son any belittling name.
He is simply busy — with a world to claim."
Then, what seemed like a few months later,
He was poised with his boxing gloves on at 16,
Ready to beat down any opponent, looking mean.
I will always remember how hard you fought
To live a productive life
The third picture of you is as a young adult.
My prayer was that I lived to see you come
Into your own
Married, children, with a loving home.
Now, as you look at me with that smile so bright,
I ask "Who" and "Why did they take your light?"
I prayed to God that the child of whoever snuffed it out
Would continue to be a blessing for them —
A child like mine
That they can be proud about.

Part IV

Will I Thank You for Your Mercies and Thank You for Your Love?

Power 'n' 24/7 Praise

Solace of an Old Friend

One day at work, I stood up in my cubicle to stretch. It was one of those full-fledged stretches with your arms to the ceiling and back arched. Those stretches feel good. But when my arms came down and my back bent back upright, my head dropped, and I felt my arms hit my desk. I saw darkness and felt my body going limp. I thought, "If I moan loud enough, maybe someone will hear, come see, and help." It worked. I heard a couple of voices call my name, and then I did not hear anything else until two male supervisors were strategizing about picking me up off the floor. The paramedics came. They took my blood pressure, which was high. It did not surprise me. I told the paramedics that my doctors (I'd had two doctors over the years since I had high blood pressure) had been trying to regulate my blood pressure. I just assumed that my pressure had gotten too high, which caused the collapse. However, the paramedics also gave me an electrocardiogram. The results of the electrocardiogram showed that further tests were necessary. Then, I had to undergo an outpatient operation that revealed I had had a heart attack sometime prior to the episode at work and now had heart disease.

That was a bit of background to bring us to this point. While driving to Bible study Wednesday evening, my chest started hurting. I had a fleeting thought not to go to class. It was a familiar pain. As long as it did not get worse, I figured I would be fine. I was glad I went, because it was a spirited discussion. However, on the way home, the familiar pains started again and continued through the night. Needless to say, I got little sleep and rest. I called into work for a sick day. Thursday, I was up and down and in and out with medicine and pain. By early Friday morning, I was doing much better. Even though I was moving slow, I was moving at a steady pace with no pain. As I got off the elevator at work, I thought, *I am not in pain. Why am I walking slower than normal? Did I come back to work too soon? Should I go home? Is it psychological? If I walked faster, will the pain will come back?*

Sitting at my desk, thinking work-related thoughts, I busied myself, taking my mind off the now-subsided pain. I was doing okay until 30 minutes into the first hour. The pain started again, at a low level. Then, the pain rapidly reached the level of Wednesday night. This time the thought of going home was an easy decision as I remembered the pain of Thursday.

I left work upset. Wow! *How do I know when to push through the pain or when to give in?* I had had a heart attack and did not even know it. *How do I know if it is just fear that is causing me to be overly cautious in dealing with a diseased heart?* Driving home, I realized I was having an anxiety attack along with my chest hurting — or could it be psychological? These were the thoughts going through my mind as I drove home, along with thoughts of early retirement, since it appeared that I could not complete a full month of work without having to be off several days. Right in the middle of the anxiety attack, I realized, "I am having an anxiety attack." Oh, no! I should not be doing this! This will be a mental and physical weakness, a stronghold for Satan, if I do not get it together spiritually! Inasmuch as the doctors had already determined it, I couldn't spiritualize away a diseased heart, but I can believe God has hold of my heart and mind! "God, my help in ages past!" *"For God has not given me the spirit of fear, but of power, love and a sound mind"!* II Timothy 1:7 Thank you, Holy Spirit!

It was clear to me that I needed help. I called my sister. Karen is a child of God. We have talked often of God and His working in our lives in various situations. I knew Karen would reach out and touch me over the phone with God's power! I knew that, in the midst of my sobbing, she could not understand what I was saying. I tried to make my voice calm and understandable and tried to leave a sensible message. I was okay that she was not able to answer. I expected her to be at work 8:30 in the morning. I left her a hopefully understandable message: "I need you, sister; I need you to pray for me and with me." I hung up, knowing she would call me as soon as she could. I started conversing with God.

By the time I got home and made it into the house, I was a lot calmer. I picked my Bible back up from where I had laid it to take off my coat. I went to a room with carpeted floors (I knew I would be down for a while), and then I dropped down to my knees. I cried, snorted, and shouted, and asked God to take away the fear. God, who is rich in mercy and infinitely longsuffering, reminded me of my morning devotion — the same devotion I had a few hours earlier when I was singing the words to the song, "How great is Thy faithfulness that every morning Thy hands have provided. GREAT, GREAT, GREAT! is Thy faithfulness, Lord, unto me. Then I started singing with words that only the Holy Spirit could understand. I was not singing in tongues, but I was crying hard and trying to sing at the same time. I was crying tears of shame, tears of repentance, and tears of joy. I ended my not-so-quiet time with one of my favorite hymns. As I was walking through the house, a thought came to my mind: "I won't need the solace of that faithful friend once I get done with the work down here." I started humming as I sat down at the computer. As I begin to write the following poem, the words jumped onto the page so fast, it seemed they were waiting to see themselves in print. I realized with a deeper conviction that God has every bit of everything under control.

Sweet Hour of Prayer Poem

I won't need you any more,
Sweet hour of Prayer
Once I get done with the work down here.
I will take this robe off and leave it in the dust
Heaven bound I'm headed
when finished with God's work I must
My heart is heavy and tired
But looking forward to helping souls
awaiting rescue from the fire
God still has work for me to do
Only, in a little while, I'll be through
Oh, sweet hour of prayer
You andI have been friends for so long
Thanks for taking me often to My Father's throne
Thank you for letting me cry in joy and in sorrow
Then drying my eyes with thoughts of the morrow
If God allows me to see another day
He will be there, too, to guide my way
Oh, what wondrous joy to talk to God in such a way
That lifts my soul to song as I pray
Sweet hour of prayer, my friend to the end
I will leave you as a new life I begin.

Thank God — Not Like Job

I thought it was because I didn't bathe as often as I should have. It was virtually impossible to drag myself into the bathroom. Lifting my legs into the tub took more energy than I had. I had just enough energy to "birdbath," hitting the vital parts. Dressing and going to work depleted what little energy I had left and me drained. God gave me what I needed to get through a day's work. I was exhausted when I arrived home. I hit the couch. By Saturday night, I seemed to have enough energy to shower and get the kids and myself ready for church on Sunday morning.

This was a continual ritual. Therefore, I wasn't surprised when small, blister-like bumps started popping up on my arms and legs — I thought it was because of bacteria on my skin. I tried home remedies that did not work. The blisters got worse. My cousin Mary, who was also my best friend, had already made plans to keep my three girls for the weekend. I dropped them off at her apartment Friday evening, showing her the blisters. My skin was so irritated that it was almost impossible to sleep. Sometime during the wee hours of the morning, I dropped off to sleep. The next morning, I woke to find my entire body covered with small, red, blister-like bumps. Later Saturday morning, the bumps started opening and secreting fluid. All I knew to do was to try to keep my skin dry by dabbing it with sterile gauze. However, the fluid started crusting and hardening. I could not lie down. My entire body was covered, except for the soles of my feet and the top of my head.

In Job 2:12, it states that Job's friends lifted up their eyes afar off, and knew him not, and they wept and rent their mantle. I looked in the mirror and cried out, "Oh, my God!" My face had swollen almost double in size and crusted over so badly that my appearance was distorted. It had had happened so fast that I didn't know what to do but call on God. I cried and read Job, who was the only one I knew who could relate to what I was going through, especially when I had to get a metal scraper to scratch the itch underneath the crusted skin. The crust had hardened so that the metal scraper only glided over the top. I had to hit the area where the itch was with the scraper to soothe the itch.

I prayed to God to help me through this and to heal me. I gently rocked back and forth, hugging myself as if it were God holding me. I sang songs of praise and talked to God, telling him that I would be strong, just like Job was. I laughed and cried as I read the book. I laughed when I got to the part about God asking Job to tell *Him* a thing or two. I was glad I could not identify with Job when he wished he had never been born. It would have taken more than boils for me to say that, as I am sure it was more than the boils that drove him to say that, but, rather, *everything* that he had gone through (the loss of his kids, for one). The depth of Job's loneliness must have been insurmountable; I still had my three beautiful daughters. I thanked God that it was only boils — and, probably, mine were milder than Job's — so I thanked God for that. Then I praised God that He counted me worthy to go through something such as Job had gone through. I thanked Him again that my situation was not like Job's. Actually, although I was in pain, God and I had the best time together. I knew I would be all right — that it was just a matter of time.

My doorbell rang. I let it ring several times, but, then, the person started banging on the door. It took me a few minutes longer than normal to get there. I was hurting when I finally muffed out a yell, "Who is it?" My brother's voice answered back. Momma had called him to stop by to see what was going on, since I was not answering the telephone and I had not called her. I cracked the door and stood back out of sight, so he could not see me. I spoke to my brother through the narrow opening. I informed him that I was okay, that I was sick but getting better, and that, no, I didn't need anything. I thanked him for stopping to check on me. I felt comfort in knowing someone cared about me.

I missed church, of course, and a couple of days of work. I spoke with my cousin, who said that she had washed my girls' clothes and would take them to school that week while I recuperated. I was free to concentrate on getting well. What really happened was that my concentration turned totally to God. The hurting propelled me into studying, praying, meditating, and singing.

One time, while singing, I laboriously walked into the bathroom, turned the shower on, and closed the bathroom door behind me as I walked out. I went back into the bedroom to get my robe (I don't know why — it hurt putting anything on). By the time I got back to the bathroom, the steam that had filled the room reminded me not to get wet. It was like my mind was on automatic pilot, which was strange, since, before, it took all my effort to even think about taking a shower. I turned the shower off. Exhausted, I sat on the toilet seat. I laughed at myself, thinking how, now, I longed for a shower. After several minutes of sitting on the toilet, I noticed a pin-head-sized crack in the crust on my left thigh. Not really thinking of what I was doing (I was still singing praises), I started picking at the crack. I was able to raise a small piece of crust and peel it off with little pain. I got so excited, I tried to pick more off — but it was too painful.

The Holy Spirit placed the thought in my mind to give myself a steam facial. I ran hot water in the face bowl. With my head practically in the bowl, I draped a towel over my head like a tent. I prayed, "Lord let it be so — let it happen, please. When I started feeling the steam through the hard crust, I started crying, but I didn't want to stop too soon. Several minutes later, I lifted my head and looked into the mirror on the wall over the face bowl. A loud, uncontrollable moan burst from my throat, and tears ran down my face and disappeared inside the opening of the rough, brown crust covering. My face stung from the tears. I cried harder because, now, I could feel them, whereas, before, the hard crust would not allow me to feel the tears.

Try to visualize being in an airplane, miles up. When you look out the window and realize you are descending. What had appeared to be mountains, with a blanket of dark rocky stuff, now look like they contain wide, flowing lines that were actually highways and roads weaving throughout the mountainous area. That is how my face looked after the steam bath. I gingerly wedged the tip of my scratching apparatus down between the cracks to uplift the crust. I first peeled the crust off around my eyes so I could see better, since my eyes were almost swollen closed; then, I peeled the rest of my face. I ran the hot water in the shower for more steam. After several minutes, I turned the water off, quickly pulled the shower curtain back to step into the bathtub, closed it, and sat down in the tub on a towel.

After a few minutes, I was able to scrape and pick larger pieces of crust off my body. It wasn't skin I was picking off, but the fluid that had crusted and layered over my skin like a hard shell. I ran out of strength (I could barely eat during the whole ordeal, so I was weak) just as the steam began to dissipate. I stepped out of the tub, dragged myself to the bedroom, and literally collapsed onto the bed, my skin burning, raw, and irritated. After I rested for about 30 minutes (too excited to wait any longer), I stepped back into the tub to start the process over again. It only took a few times rotating from bath to bed; it seemed as soon as the air got underneath the crust, it loosened up and almost fell off with little effort from my now swift-and-efficient picking skills. The places on my skin that once were small blisters had merged to become blotches of deflated (some still had fluid in them) dark, wrinkled skin. I prayed myself to sleep with tears of thanksgiving and woke the next morning for the first time in several days from a full night's sleep. I looked at my body. Though the dark blotches that covered my body were ugly, they had started to dry up.

When I thought I looked well enough not to scare people, I called the dermatologist. I was able to get in that next day. The doctor stated they (people in his profession) did not know what caused the blisters. They knew it was a genetic disease that lay dormant until something (they don't know what) causes it to manifest. I asked him if the catalyst could have been bacteria on the skin from not keeping clean. I was so embarrassed and ashamed for not showering routinely that I braced myself, waiting for him to say, "Yes," which would affirm that I had brought the affliction on myself. However, he said, "No." The trigger would have been something internal. He stated the medical name, but, since then, I have forgotten it. I got a prescription filled and went home. My cousin kept the girls the remainder of the week so I could rest.

What happened to me is something I seldom speak of — not because people would or would not believe — but because I am humbled to receive what God allowed me to go through as a transformation process. He chose me to see if I would keep the faith and run *to* Him! Why would He do this for me? If for nothing else, to anchor my faith. Only God knows what trials and tribulations you must face to make your foundation unshakable. Today, I still have some spots, which, though faded, remind me of how wonderfully gracious and caring God is.

Power 'n' 24/7 Praise

I Am Healed, and Everything Is Well

"What's going on?" was the voice on the other end of the phone.

I was so glad to hear my sister's voice that I blurted out praises to God. Then rattled off why I had called, ending with "I know my sister will pray for me and pray with me." No seconds elapsed before the voice on the other end was in bold prayer. Sister reached out and laid her hands on me. God, through Karen, blessed my core. I could not stop to listen to her, because, by then, my spirit was again in communion with God, and I was in high praise.

Every now and then, I heard, "Hallelujah — no weapon formed against Her will prosper … Satan attempts but knows he cannot win against a child of God … casting down imagination and every high thing that exalteth itself against the knowledge of God — Hallelujah!

We are more than conquerors. God still has work for her to do…"

I could not tell where the praises stopped and the prayers started. We continued several more minutes, and then she said, "I am in the bathroom at work, and I have to get back. We have touched and agreed … Believe you are healed, and everything is well." I said, "I am healed, and everything is well … and I received it.

Holding Tight To Reality

Reality, for me,
is knowing that the promises I read
Each day are mine.
I don't forget now and then
To remember back, to remind myself,
of the black days, the dark days
Virtually no friends
Lonely singleness, three children,
Facing the reality of probable homelessness
Then a second marriage to a drug-filled life
Instead of a 180, a 360 to singleness and strife.
Now nurturing five on a dime.
Struggling, yet prevailing one day at a time,
Holding tight to promises I read each day
Through years of tears, not giving up, not giving in
Fighting thoughts of suicide
Fighting thoughts of solicitation
I find refuge in His pavilion
Loving my kids, loving my God, holding on
To promises I read each day
I don't forget now and then to remember
Back to the black days, the dark days, that now
Hold a glimmering speck that keeps me holding on
Because the promises I read each day are real.

Anchoring Faith

There are times when my faith is not so certain, solid, and unshakeable. These are the times I reach for the Bible to remind myself of all the promises God has given me, such as the scripture in *I Peter 1:3-9; Blessed be the God and Father of our Lord Jesus Christ, which according to his abundant mercy hath begotten us again unto a lively hope by the resurrection of Jesus Christ from the dead, to an inheritance incorruptible, and undefiled, and that fadeth not away, reserved in heaven for you, who are kept by the power of God through faith unto salvation ready to be revealed in the last time. Wherein ye greatly rejoice, though now for a season, if need be, ye are in heaviness through manifold temptations: that the trial of your faith, being much more precious than of gold that perisheth, though it be tried with fire, might be found unto praise and honour and glory at the appearing of Jesus Christ: whom having not seen, ye love; in whom, though now ye see him not, yet believing, ye rejoice with joy unspeakable and full of glory: receiving the end of your faith, even the salvation of your souls.*

Looking back, I cannot remember — even once — doubting who God is. I doubted *myself* plenty of times. In fact, low self-esteem has been a thorn in my flesh since I was about 11, when big Marta Grisbee beat me up in the classroom in front of about 20 kids. When I got up from the floor where Big Marta had laid me out, the kids teased me about the grease spot left. They called me "grease monkey" and "tar baby." They knew as well as I that all of us had to use grease for the skin ash. So, why they teased me about that, I don't know. My friends told me that I was brave to fight back; everyone took Marta's side because they were afraid of her. Marta was three shades darker, fifty pounds heavier, and two feet taller than me. Though she shook me like a "rag doll", I had fingernails, whereas she didn't. Her arms were scratched up pretty bad. But, I wasn't embarrassed by the fight; I was deflated by the taunting of my peers. To this day, I remember how the after-effects of that fight made me feel so insignificant. The effects were still taking a toll on my emotions years later, and that caused me to ask the question, "How does this have anything to do with anchoring faith?"

Children are so impressionable. Things that seem of no consequence are burnt into their psyche deeper than a parent could imagine. Can we, as parents, control what could be a life-altering experience for our children? Can we control the positive or negative aspect of an experience? Many things determine one's faith. Continually relating how a potentially negative experience can be a positive one if controlled by godly attributes can be effective in establishing a strong, life-altering faith.

Because of the thorn in my flesh, my goal was to edify my children in feeling good about themselves. Once I started digging myself out of the self-pitying state I was in, I had to learn not to beat and bruise my children with my tongue and loud voice. I had to learn to temper my tongue by speaking to them with kindness, appreciation, encouragement, and character-building words instead of negative and demeaning words. I didn't realize that I was not honoring God by not being thankful and by not treating the children He had blessed me with as He would want me to treat them.

You tell yourself you don't mistreat your kids, but you really do. For instance, when you are mad, you speak ugliness to them by telling them to shut up, shouting at them, and spanking them when you are angry, just to name a few things. You don't take the time to think how they are not yours but God's and that it is God who allows you to watch over, to protect, to teach, and to love them. They can't fight back when you rant, rave, and yell. But they can run away, and sometimes they do, all while their young minds are being branded and seared with negative experience that can haunt, hurt, and hinder their future.

You know, your children love you, and it takes a lot for them to stop loving you — if they ever do. Mine loved me through all I did or didn't do when I should have. If I could have a "do-over" and give them back the childhood I took away from them, I would. Maybe you will cry, as I did, when you read their stories. However, I appreciate them for who they are. I thank them for loving me and showing their love to me in so many ways. I am thankful for God's grace and mercy to allow me to learn — while they were young — how vitally important my treatment of them would affect their future and the life of their children.

Throughout my adult life, God and my children were my only consistent presence. Every ounce of my being was dedicated to loving God and my children. A loving home makes all the difference in the world to impressionable children longing to be loved and needing to know that they have a special place in the family. We could not go many places, but we certainly had fun at home, being a family. We have a God-given commandment to do those things to nourish an anchoring faith in our children.

I am thankful to God that there are many more loving, kind, and considerate parents than there are not. My prayer is that the generational blessings of fruit from responsible parents will continue to abound. God gave me a bonus — plus a second chance — to do it right. Because of my loving children, my 11 grandkids are terrific!

Power 'n' 24/7 Praise

Life's Presence

Young, innocent, and trusting; we walk with our hands tightly gripped by stronger hands. We see not or could care less of the weights waiting patiently to have their turn to burden us down. Carefree and clueless of the pressures soon to be thrust upon us, we revel in life and do all we are brave enough to do, with no thought of the hand that once so tightly gripped ours. To some degree, great or small, we rebel restlessly against the established order — the very thing that keeps us from freedom of irresponsible self-expression and diving off cliffs of undetermined heights.

We often take leaps of stupidity, leaps of uncertainties, and yes, even what could be considered leaps of faith. As we tumble through corridors of time, we glimpse fleeting rays of sunlight when — for what seems only seconds in life — we feel the warmth, and we feel the love and realize we are not alone. Wow! Someone knows how we feel — and understands us.

An invisible hand gently cradles and soothes, briefly interrupting the downward spiral. Slowly, we fall through dark dispensations of life. But now we have more knowledge, we have an awareness of presence. We are strengthened by the fact that there are bigger, stronger hands that have tempered our falling headfirst through life. We now have hope and a sense of balance. We are able to reach out and grab a hand. It is smaller. We can engulf it, hold it, cradle it. Life has not yet roughened or toughened this hand. Let us grip it tight.

Power 'n' 24/7 Praise

Memories from Charlotte

With innocent eyes, I stare out the public transportation bus window, waiting to see the downtown skyline appear at the horizon. I glance over to make sure that my younger siblings are still by my side, behaving studiously. Today we meet our mother for lunch at her office building in Crown Center. The eagerness of being with my mom while she is in a rosy disposition gives me an excited anxiousness. A flock of butterflies has taken flight in my stomach. As our stop approaches, I tell my sisters to get ready to get off. I carefully inspect our faces, hair, and limbs for anything stray or ashen, securing a sense that we're looking our Sunday best and wanting to guarantee that our mother's pride is front and center when it comes to her daughters.

I can't wait to see the smile on her face as her co-workers become enthused about how we've grown or how pretty we're becoming. It's a smile that we get to see only in public, because she does not smile like that within the walls of our residence. Deeply, I exhale as we make our way across the street and into the skyscraper. I know that smile will find its home on her beautiful face only periodically over the next sixty minutes, and then it will be extinguished by the overwhelming spirit of depression that has rested upon my mother for so many reasons that can't be comprehended by a child's mind.

I didn't know that my mother suffers from this illness. All I knew is that, when she was home, she slept a lot, tired from working. As my mother's oldest child, I handled a lot of responsibilities for her. So I try to do exactly what she says so she can rest, because maybe, one day, she will be rested and not sleep the evening away but spend it with us. Day after day, we sit at her feet or play in her hair while she sleeps. Once I reached adolescence, she shared with me that she suffered from depression. I think to myself, "When? How? Why?" The stories she shared with me jog my memory, and I silently thank God that He didn't take her from me and my siblings. Although depression weaves itself through my childhood and attempted to make me a motherless child, I know that my mother did her best. She suffered in silence and defeated depression the same way.

Today, I see a woman who was triumphant over depression, with God's grace. She has embraced her life and allowed God's love to saturate her, turning her into a jovial, free, and giving spirit to whom others look for inspiration. Long gone are the days that were dominated by depression. She welcomes life and strives to meet the purpose God has set for her.

Charlotte Dupree

Memories from Carla

I remember when I was a little girl, my mother, my sisters, myself, and sometimes my Grandmother, would go to yard sales and estate sales. It was like treasure hunting. We would shop for treasures in other people's trash, and we would go home and furnish our home. It was so exciting to get what, to us, looked like new stuff — for cheap. I really enjoyed junking (that is what we called it) as a little girl, and, still, to this day, I love *DISCOUNTS*!

Carla

Memories from Caira

Even though I was able to witness such a strong work ethic from my mother, her overloaded work schedule often affected her relationship with her children. She was often too tired from her workday to bond with her children. My siblings and I often had to take care of ourselves, cook for ourselves, and clean for ourselves, because my mother was too tired from work. I believe this way of being brought up still affects us all to this day. I also believe this may explain a lot of why our family is not as close in relationship with one another as we probably could be. We never learned how to "live as a family." But, by the grace of God, we are still alive and living according to the leading of the Holy Spirit, who is the teacher of all things.

Praise be to God, my mother always was sure to teach us the word of God. She instilled God's word in us as children. And because of her Biblical teachings, I will never stray from having a relationship with Jesus Christ. I thank God for my mother often. And, although there were some things she could have done better, she did not do everything wrong! My parents got divorced when I was born. I was raised in a household of six people without a father as a role model. At the age of 30, I can honestly look back and say that my mother raised me and my siblings to the best of her ability. She had to work hard to maintain our living (utilities, rent, food, personal needs, etc). My mother sometimes worked overtime or part time on other jobs in order to maintain a single-parent household with five children.

On many occasions, my mother was very flexible with me having "sleepovers" with my friends on weekends. Our house was always the house for fun, laughter, and freedom. Many of my childhood friends were in very awkward situations with their individual family members, so my house was always the "getaway" house. Our house was always the house that many of my friends could come to have fun and get their minds away from the horrible things that were going on with their individual families. Our house was always the house that was used as a source of freedom. There were many weekend sleepovers. My mother would make sure we had food in the household for taco salad, rotel dip, and a pancake breakfast. I can still see all the bodies sleeping on the floor with many blankets and pillows. I can still see all my friends and me in the kitchen, cutting tomatoes and slicing lettuce and mixing ground beef for taco salad. This was always one of the many joys of my childhood. I thank God that my mother was always open to having my friends over. She did not mind being the mother for all five of her own children and my many other friends who constantly used our house for fun, laughter, and freedom. Thanks, Mom!

Caira Dean

Memories from Russell

My mother is one of the hardest-working people I know. Growing up as a child, I witnessed her getting up very early every morning and going to work. It was very rare for her to miss work. Her motivation was generated by the needs of all her children. All five children were different in talents, and, therefore, all had different needs. We each needed our own share of support, inspiration, and encouragement. I viewed my mother as a multitalented woman. She was able to provide all of us children all of the confidence and inspiration we needed.

I remember sharing bedrooms, riding the Metro bus, and wearing Payless shoes. I remember Christmases, some better than others. I remember summers with my brother and me and my sisters watching us because our mother was working. My brother and I did what boys did, and sometimes my sisters whipped us with switches. My brother and I refused to have two mamas, so it was very challenging at times for my sisters and us. It was challenging for my sisters who were in and out of the role of sisters to be mother, and for us, in and out of the role of their children and brothers.

Once, they were going to whip us, but we ran through the house and out the front door. We didn't think about the fact that we would have to come back home. We finally realized this was the reason they didn't chase after us. We waited until the minute before momma came home — we thought that by then it would be too late for our sisters to whip us. We might as well get one whipping by mom instead of two. The plan did work as far as one whipping. Momma was too tired to whip. She gave us a scowling tongue lash and sent us to our room for the rest of the evening. The next day, when mom left, our sisters pulled out the switches.

Russell

Memories from Ricky

To My Mother
    "All I really remember as a child when it comes to my mother is that, no matter what I did, she was always there for me every time I messed up and did something crazy. And I was always into some trouble. I never stopped moving, and she didn't either!"

(Written by Ricky at the age of 19)

PART V

Yes, I will Worship You, Lord, as the Great "I Am"

Power 'n' 24/7 Praise

Ultimate Praise

It's quiet time.
I'm reading how it will be in heaven
when, suddenly without warning or thought,
my face goes ugly, tears dropping hard and fast,
lips turned down, quivering
the kind of ugly you get when every
emotion in your body bursts forth,
coming through your face,
when every emotion bursts forth through your arms
You throw up your hands to the heavens
and you shout "GLORY!"
Yep, that's me in my quiet time
That all of a sudden,
out of nowhere
is not quiet any longer.
Yep, that's me
Ms. Unemotional Picture of Piety
sampling how it will be
praising God throughout eternity.

My God Ring

One day at work, a co-worker approached me with a surprising and humbling question. "What is going on with you?" I had let my appearance slip down to a level not normal for me. Rona could ask me this because she is one of the few people I knew was genuinely concerned about me and who would inconvenience herself, if it took that, to help me. I had, about a week before, questioned my own self about my appearance, telling myself to get it together. God had brought me through the death of my son several months before, but, now, I had to handle the ache of loneliness that death had left. Intellectually, I handled death, and spiritually, I handled death, but the reality of knowing Ricky would never again do this or do that took my emotions longer to grasp.

I had predictable periods of crying and needing to be alone and needing not to be alone. I definitely had periods of not wanting to do anything. I had a job, and I knew I needed to keep my job, so I moved robotically, doing what was necessary. My fingers still typed on the keyboard. It didn't matter what my cuticles looked like. My teeth were brushed, but it didn't matter if I wore lipstick. My clothes were clean, but it wasn't necessary that they matched or were stylish. My hair wasn't looking bad — just pulled back in a short, two-inch ponytail that stuck straight out because of the type of hair style I wear. There was no need for earrings or any other jewelry. I was content moving about in a detached state.

I knew I was slipping, and I knew what awaited me at the end of the slip. I had been there before. God had sent a reminder through Rona, who jarred me mentally to inhale the fresh air of awareness of the Holy Spirit working in my life with joy and peace, and exhale the spirit of sorrow, self-pity, and guilt. This knowledge made an immediate change in me and in my appearance. However, I felt I needed a visual reminder of who I am in God and all that I was destined to be, especially through the hard times of life.

One day, I was flipping through an Avon book and saw a single-band silver-tone filigree ring. It was a simple ring with a lace pattern and three very small diamond-look accents going across the top. I thought it was the perfect ring to remind myself of who I am in Christ. Having experience with Avon's jewelry, I knew this ring would last without turning my finger green. I ordered it. Two weeks later, a co-worker delivered my precious order. I waited until I arrived home, and then I had a humbling quiet time of praise and prayer with God, recommitting my love to Him. I slipped the ring on the third finger of my left hand as a visual symbol of my love for God, which calls me to present my body as a living sacrifice, holy and acceptable to God. I look at this ring and remind myself that I am royalty and that my soul was purchased at a precious price. I will treat myself as a child of God.

Has this visual aid helped? Yes! I have worn my "God Ring" for more than a year now. I did not slip back; I wear my heels at times, my earrings and makeup, and I have dropped 20 pounds. I have a new resolve. I am a fine, spirit-filled Christian lady, full with joy for Christ. But, I am not fine because of what I wear or put on — I am fine because I am growing closer to the image of Christ. I now strive daily with my focus on life, not death. Christ says, "I am life — the light of men." In Christ, there is no darkness, no death — only life.

As I turn my ring back and forth on my finger, I smile. The infinity of the circle symbolizes my life in Christ. Yes, I am royalty and soon to be part of the royal marriage feast. Then, I will no longer need this earthly, visual reminder.

Endless Ecstasy

Have you heard?
A good marriage should be
like friendship on steroids.
Is there such a thing?
This is rare — with so many
relationships full of lust and passion
ending in "shotgun" marriages
for morality's satisfaction
Well, there will be
no more brief snatches and glimpses
of breathless feel-goods.
This commitment was made with no hesitation
A marriage to God
makes a sure reservation
for a lifetime of faithfulness
and satisfaction,
and eternity, where pure praise
is an ongoing action
This ring, placed on the third finger of my left hand,
Is a thing of beauty — an endless band,
an outward symbol woven to show no end
of love for one's best friend
A love
With no pretense of happiness, no façade
Married to one's best friend, married to God
Only joy of endless ecstasy
A happy forever-after beginning
Of ultimate praise and jubilance

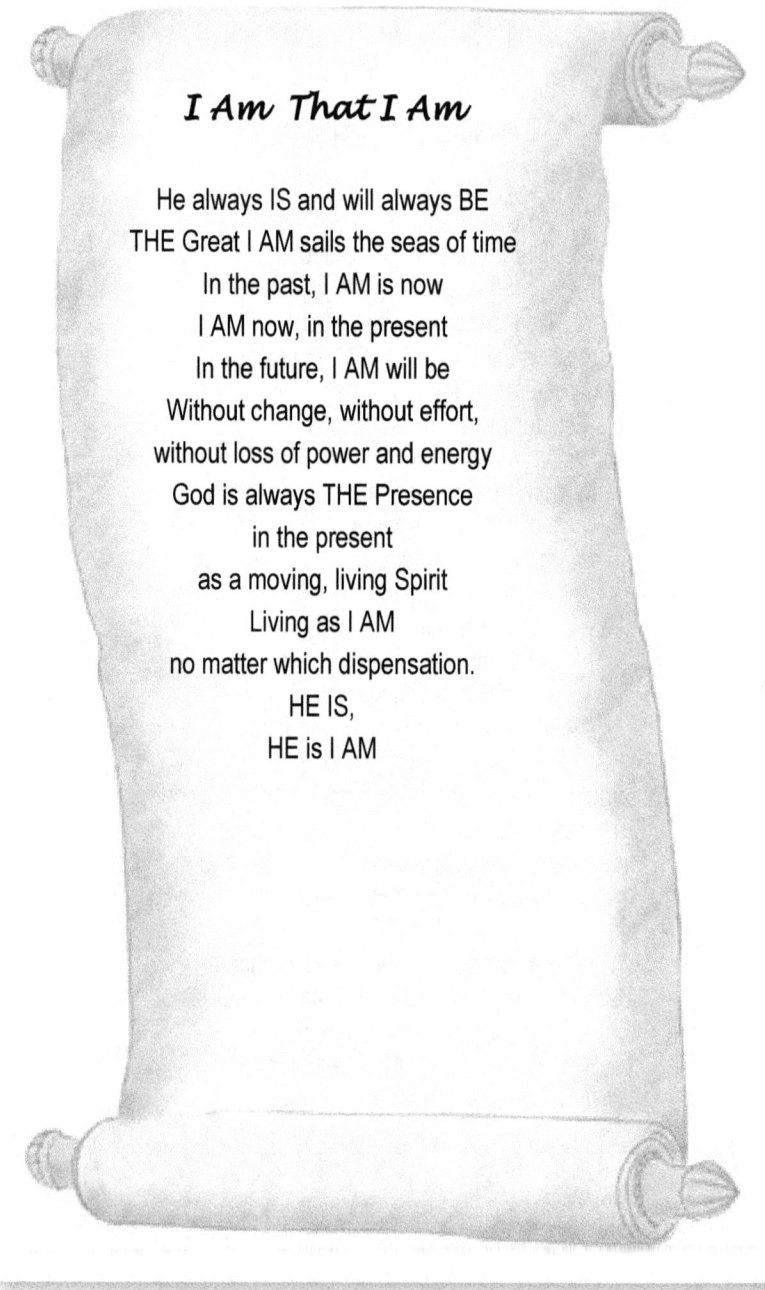

I Am That I Am

He always IS and will always BE
THE Great I AM sails the seas of time
In the past, I AM is now
I AM now, in the present
In the future, I AM will be
Without change, without effort,
without loss of power and energy
God is always THE Presence
in the present
as a moving, living Spirit
Living as I AM
no matter which dispensation.
HE IS,
HE is I AM

Elect

I was predetermined as a perfect plan
designed by God's hand
though death tried to steal me away in infancy
pneumonia, whooping cough, mumps, or chicken pox
all within the same few weeks
sending me into a coma deep —
this, too, was part of God's plan
to show that He can
Specially conceived for the Master's need
as a perfect plan from His hand
Life's weight too heavy to take
attempted suicide failed
God's plan prevailed
Infections permeated my being
evoking a second coma
through Christ's blood — a sweet aroma
God spoke, "The thoughts I have of you are as the sands,
My love for you breaks death's bands"
I awake to a plan that is not of man
I am an over-comer here for God's purpose
A silent heart attack that left
me with a resolve to work while it's day
Death's failures to steal me away
further assure
busy I will be until God's plan for me
has come to an end
Then, and only then, with death used as
a stepping-stone to a new life
Will I begin
Yes, we all are predetermined as a perfect plan
chosen by God's sovereign hand
Are you a believer?
Then you are an Elect
chosen to help effect
God's master PLAN

I Will Praise You, Lord

And I will praise You, Lord, for all of my days
And I will praise You, Lord, for keeping me in Your way
And I will praise You, Lord, for blessings from above
Thank You for your mercies
and thank You for Your love
Once held in bondage from Christ's liberties
Blind from knowing the depth of Christ's love for me
Satan had a stronghold that weakness could not free
Years of fruitless labor salvation to achieve
But one day,
Through God's grace and favor,
someone took my hand and
Showed me in the Scripture God's true salvation plan
Now I follow God instead of prideful man
I am set free — set free
to seek and understand
That God wants me in Him only to believe
the Eternal Godhead is pure sovereignty
To live this life in faithfulness,
heaven to achieve
quickened and regenerated
by His wisdom divine
growing stronger in power, love, and sound mind
sanctified in Christ, called to be a saint
clothed in full armor a soldier who will not faint
translated from darkness into the marvelous light
pressing forward in battle,
strengthened by God's might
I am set free — set free
And I will praise You, Lord, for all of my days
And I will praise You, Lord,
for keeping me in Your way
And I will praise You, Lord, for blessings from above
Thank You for Your mercies, and thank You for Your love.

True Worship

It could be once a week to meet and greet
for purpose of edifying and exhorting each
to love with all the admonition from above
But to put on and never take off is a continual
wearing of garments of praise that is worn
day to day ...
a refueling and re-strengthening
a crucifying and self-denying
a casting down of imaginings
transforming and conforming
a conscious walking in the Holy Spirit of God
It's not a once-a-week, occasional thing, it's
a daily wearing of
thankfulness and praise
gratitude and humility,
joy and love,
obedience and sacrifice.
To be in the image of Christ
is not an occasional thing — it's a way of life

About the Author

Janice Revels is a native of Kansas City, Missouri. She discovered writing as a teenager when she developed her Young Adult BTU (Baptist Training Union) class first newsletter. Later, as founder and editor of Christian Sisters News magazine, Janice published her poems and articles with other inspired writers who volunteer their talents to her venture in spreading the gospel of Jesus Christ through five states. Janice is currently the Administrative Support for her church while ministering in the area of discipleship. Her passion is serving God, loving Him and being loved by Him. Janice is the mother of five wonderful children who has blessed her with eleven super-wonderful grandchildren.

www.ingramcontent.com/pod-product-compliance
Lightning Source LLC
Chambersburg PA
CBHW050557300426
44112CB00013B/1965